Do the Hustle Without the Hassle

A Quick, Simple Affordable Way to Make Money at Age 45+

Angela Heath

TKC Productions and Printing
College Park, MD

Dedication:

Soli Deo Gloria

Acknowledgements

To my son, Tarik A. Green, you are my second love. Your strength and faith encourages me to keep going no matter what. Keep hustling son. Remember, you are a gift to mankind.

Dalton Phillips, my faithful friend, your edit job set me on the right path after being led astray. Then Brenda Siler came along and polished the manuscript with her special touches. I am grateful to you both for your responsiveness to my last minute requests.

I thank Vicky Spriggs for putting up with my intense focus and failure to attend to things at home. Your friendship is special.

To my sister, Carolyn Slade, one of my biggest fans and best friends. Your patience with me is noted and greatly appreciated. Love you much.

To the Kingdom Wealth Builders and Investor Prayer Group, this is a result of the 90 days of GPS. Your prayers are so strong and productive. Thank you. Keep believing.

Joel, thanks for getting this piece finally published!

To the 45+ year old readers, you are a rare gem. You bring wisdom and insight to work that can only be gained by the passage of time. Use your talents and skills to define work according to your own terms. Happy hustle!

Table of Contents

Part III: Proceed

Bonus Materials

Part I: Poised

A dignified, self-confident manner or bearing;
Composure (dictionary.com)

CHAPTER 1

Introduction

What does "do the hustle" mean? It's not the popular dance from the 1970's; it's not taking advantage or swindling someone for a living. Instead, it is leveraging 21st century tools on your own to make more money – part time or full time, you decide.

I wrote this book for a specific group of people, those who are 45 years of age and older. These are people who want to know THE quickest, simplest, most affordable way to make money online without much hassle. They are ready to do their own thing and earn income as soon as possible. However, they are not interested in learning about domain names, web hosting, HTML, payment gateways or hiring tech staff to sit by their sides.

Is this you?

In this resource, you will find step-by-step instructions for ONE WAY to leverage your existing talents, skills and passions without blowing your retirement income or maxing out credit cards. Although there are many ways to make money online, this book covers the simplest, quickest, most affordable way. The learning curve is short because you build on what you already know. However, there will be some new skills to be learned.

But before I reveal this ONE WAY to earning income on the Internet, let me further explain a few things to help you determine if you should bother reading this book. (Turn to Chapter 3 if you must know what the ONE WAY is right now). If you find that this book is not for you but you have already purchased it, why not gift it to a friend?

First, you may be wondering why this book is written for people age 45 and older. Of course, the techniques I teach work for anyone, of any age. But the book targets mature workers for four reasons.

Why Age 45?

First, age discrimination in the workplace is real. Believe it or not, there is actually a law that forbids it, the Age Discrimination in Employment Act of 1967. At age 40, it is illegal for employers to judge you based on your age and not your abilities.

Nonetheless, you and I both know it happens every day. In fact, it might be impacting you now if you have lost your job or can't find a better one.

Far too often, mature workers are laid off when a corporation downsizes. Sure, companies may want to trim their labor costs by replacing the highest paid employees with less expensive staff. But sometimes these choices are made based on negative stereotypes about workers who are too old, too slow, behind the technological times and unwilling to learn.

These are simply myths.

Once laid off, it can take you almost a year to find a new job. The older you get, the worse it is. In fact, in December 2017, the Bureau of Labor Statistics Employment Situation Report notes that job seekers ages 55 to 64 were unemployed for over eight months, 34 weeks[1].

According to the AARP Public Policy Institute, a stunning third of job seekers ages 55+ are considered long-term unemployed[2] (out of work for 27 weeks or more). If you were unemployed six months or more, what could you do to survive? If you don't know, read on.

Unless you have a substantial stash to sustain you, which the average American does not have, being out of work so long would be extremely stressful and life-altering. You could find yourself bankrupt, homeless, and hopeless.

Second, during my recent travels, I have interviewed and read about far too many brilliant, experienced workers who are under-employed. I define under-employed as either super bored at work or grossly under paid. What a waste!

Those who I interviewed told me they were looking for the path to self-expression for profit. When you know you are capable of more but the opportunity to express your true genius and passion remains elusive, it drains your soul. It's dreadful. The pay check helps but it doesn't cure the heart cry. I know; I've been there.

When you reach age 45, you often evaluate how far you have climbed the corporate ladder. If your promotions were limited and your boss minimized your contribution, you feel frustrated. In addition, looking back over your life, it is normal to search for meaning and purpose. Some people will not find it expressed in their lives and careers.

Third, there are few things more disheartening than being vastly underpaid. If this is your experience, your needs and desires are put on pause; I am sure you've grown tired of living on "Barely Get Along Street," right next to "Grumble Alley." You deserve to be compensated fairly, but if your manager does not think so, you may want to promote yourself.

Finally, this book speaks to people age 45 and older because the technology revolution continues to change everything. If in two years a smart phone becomes outdated, can you imagine how outdated knowledge and procedures are from 20, 30 or 40 years ago?

It's time to re-tool.

You must learn to leverage 21st century technology to get ahead of where the market clearly is going. If you don't, you will be left behind. This book outlines the quickest, simplest, most affordable way to do so.

Should I Bother Reading This Book?

Before you invest your time and money, I want you to be clear: If you are age 45 or older, given the information I shared above, **you should continue reading this book** if you can locate yourself within the following scenarios:

- You doubt that you can make money doing something you like.
(See - Renewing Your Mind, Chapter 4)
- You are not a computer geek but you want to make extra money on the side.
(See – The Tools You Will Need, Chapter 6)
- You want your children to help you make money online.
(See – Tips for Doing the Hustle with Millennial Children, Bonus Materials)

- You have always wanted to own your own business but you don't know anything about it.
  (See – The Business Side of Profit, Chapter 5)
- You want to make money doing something different but you are not quite sure what you can do.
  (See – GIG Assessment, Chapter 7)
- You have been thinking about offering a service online but want to test the waters before you waste your time, energy and savings.
  (See –Which Gig Sites Work Best for You, Chapter 8)
- You are ready to start but you want a mentor to guide you.
  (See – Mentoring and Training, Bonus Materials)

This resource **may not be what you need** if your expectations are much different from the intent of this book. Let me be **clear**, if you can locate yourself in one or more of the following scenarios, **this book is not for you. Why not gift it to a friend?**

- You are interested in a get rich quick scheme that guarantees your success (no one can guarantee you anything; results depend on your efforts).
- You do not want to work at all (sorry I can't help you with that).
- You have no desire to learn anything new (you will use what you already know, but you also need to learn a new way of work).
- You have no interest in online tools and opportunities (this is not the book for you).
- You need someone to give you daily directives (sorry you must work without supervision unless you seek out additional training or mentoring).

- You want a full time job with benefits (this is not the book for you).
- You want to learn about every possible way to make money online (we advise you to test one system to make money at a time. You can add more money making options over time).

How this Book is Organized.

In summary, **Do the Hustle Without the Hassle** is a resource to help you renew your mindset for the changing way of work; assess your potential gig opportunities; guide you in business logistics; and provide one of the most comprehensive listings of gig websites.

Part I: Poised, outlines the context for understanding the gig economy. It stresses the importance of the right mindset, so you can approach the digital space with more confidence.

Part II: Primed, prepares you to be smart about participating in the online marketplace. You will have more clarity as you create a workable plan for success.

Part III: Proceed, contains the most comprehensive listing of the digital marketplace you will find. Many people are tempted to start here. If you do, you will miss some valuable insights and tools that are truly beneficial. All three sections of this book are important for success.

Whether you are interested in online gig work as a stop-gap measure to pay the rent right now or you never want to work for anyone else again, **Do the Hustle Without the Hassle** can help.

My Story.

Let me share a little of my story with you. Years ago, I was fired from a good paying job. I was ashamed. I didn't have much savings because I had recently purchased my first property. However, because of my faith, I never fretted.

Being unemployed gave me the time I needed to write my first book, which led to a second and a third. These books opened doors for a thriving consulting practice that took off slowly, but resulted in a six figure income. I was set free from the drudgery of the "normal" and released into a life work that I loved. You can do the same.

For over 20 years, I have enjoyed a healthy measure of success. I travelled to forty-five states across the country speaking and training. Working with clients, I produced approximately 75 program kits, engagement campaigns, booklets and pamphlets. My company was responsible for clients winning five national awards, and I have been interviewed on several television and radio programs.

My name has been mentioned in newspapers and magazines across the country. I even had the pleasure of speaking at an international conference in South Africa!

After building this successful consulting practice, catastrophic illness hit my family not once, but twice. The demands of caregiving limited the amount of travel and work I could do. I didn't want to fly around the country and leave my sweet baby boy alone.

Leukemia demanded my presence at the hospital and eventually the cancer clinic. I was there more than I was at home. So, I put the company on pause. (Actually, the company permanently closed but I didn't realize that at the beginning.)

The first battle with cancer lasted three and a half years. I didn't work much for about two years. I used my savings, investments, insurance, my son's college fund and retirement account to survive. I had so little money that I lost my way and was forced into slave labor. (I took a part-time job in a very oppressive government environment.) I called this period of life my "insane asylum days" because I had to be insane to work in that place!

The manager was incompetent, I had no freedom of expression and I was paid far less than I deserved. Have you ever been there?

The first year after leaving that oppressive part-time job, I tripled my income consulting as I had done for years before. But I constantly searched for new ways to earn income. I had a burning desire to stop trading time for dollars because I had already lived through the disastrous impact of having limited time.

Frustrated, I began exploring ways to make money on-line, fumbling around for seven long years losing money and wasting time. I met others my age who were struggling and trying to make money online and offline, and I began mentoring and training them. I was well on my way to establishing a new business that could feed my soul, utilize my best skills and make a profit at the same time.

Then, my son relapsed and several months later had a bone marrow transplant. We were in the hospital for six months and recovering at home for about six more months. Again, I did not work for about a year. But I read everything I could about the gig economy, learned what people want to know and conducted my own research.

I figured out a business model, built a team and began to make a profit. I combined my gifts, talents and passions (public speaking, training and resource development) to offer corporations and consumers thought leadership and tools to leverage the gig economy. In this book, I will show you how to use the same process.

Seriously, I am no different from you. I made a lot of mistakes and wasted much time mired in a fog of confusion. I wish I could show you a YouTube video of my seven years of frustration, with all of the tears, disappointments, and major blunders. You will never have this experience if you start with the online gig work as taught in this book.

Living my story led me to write this book. Mature people kept coming to me to help them hustle. Some complained that they didn't want the hassle, some were averse to the risk of losing their money; others did not want to manage employees. They all wanted something simple and quick. This resource is in direct response to what the market requested.

I know *Do the Hustle Without the Hassle* will help you; it focuses on ONE quick, simple and affordable way to get started in the gig economy. There are many other options for gig work that I teach. Once you get started, the opportunities are unlimited.

Happy hustle.

References:

[1] "Employment Situation Summary." U.S. Bureau of Labor Statistics. Accessed February 05, 2018. https://www.bls.gov/news.release/empsit.nr0.htm.

[2] "Unemployment rate for those ages 55 increases in December." AARP. Accessed February 05, 2018. http://blog.aarp.org/2018/01/05/unemployment-rate-for-those-ages-55-increases-in-december/.

CHAPTER 2

Back to the Future: Your Ability to Earn is Rooted in The Past

What finished product or service can you offer in the marketplace? Do you know what makes your heart sing? As a mentor, I ask these types of questions all the time. Frequently, I get responses like, "I really don't know." Or, even worse, "I don't know what anyone would pay me for besides what I do now to earn a living."

I am always saddened when I hear this because my motto is, "You can't live 45-plus years without having something to offer in the marketplace. It's simply impossible." But, then I remember this inability to see what you can produce and sell is actually rooted in historical events and socialization that took place way before you were born. Generation after generation has been taught the same.

This chapter explores the economic and social trends that have limited your perceptions of yourself. You are a victim of real identity theft when you don't know what you can offer to add value to others. You will think back to your early years and restore to life wonderful possibilities once you understand how your value was silenced, then you can more easily recapture it.

Economic Trends and You

Prior to the industrial revolution, most people lived in small rural communities. Life was subsistence living, meaning families produced enough food and clothing for the survival of their group. They also bartered with other families.

Some developed a "side hustle" of selling a small portion of their crops or weaving clothes to sell. Others were more enterprising as skilled craftsmen like carpenters, iron and masonry workers. The work was hard but everyone knew what they could produce to sell on their own.

During the 18th and 19th centuries, our nation moved primarily from being an agricultural rural society to becoming industrialized cities. The large manufacturing of goods fueled this change. We were taught to depend upon this model.

People flocked from the country to the cities to earn income. At this time, people began to bury their creative abilities. There was no space to display them at the local factory. Repetitive, mindless piecemeal work started where no one employee owned the entire process of manufacturing from beginning to end. Therefore, it became more difficult for the average worker to sell their skill set outside the factory.

Company towns were built to supply everything the employees needed. In some companies, employees were never paid wages, but received scrip instead, a form of credit to purchase over-priced items in the company stores. They often provided substandard housing and schools for their employees' children. People increasingly became dependent on their employers.

The service economy followed shifting us from primarily producing goods to primarily providing services. Consequently, there was a massive decline in availability of low-skill jobs and a higher demand for college educated knowledge workers.

Currently, we are in the digital information age and the on-demand economy or the gig economy. Again, work has dramatically been restructured, resulting in an increased reliance on computerization, robotics and information. The speed of technology and fast foods suggests that you can have what you want, when you want it. Automation is replacing more and more people. The gig economy is growing exponentially.

Those who are digital dinosaurs will soon become extinct. Does this refer to you?

The Original

I love watching children play. They tend to dream huge dreams. A boy might be the dragon-slaying prince with the most powerful sword. A little girl may pretend to be a fairy princess who rides on the wings of a magical butterfly. They are always the fastest, biggest, and smartest in their own minds until someone tells them that they are not.

However, the one game I have never seen kids play is the game of failure. Have you ever witnessed kids slowdown in a race so they can be the last across the finish line? Have you ever seen a kid who loves soccer hide so he can be overlooked for the team? No, it doesn't happen. Kids believe they are special. If they mess up, they believe they should get a do over.

You were created as a one of a kind masterpiece. There has never been, and there will never be another person like you. You are priceless. Your exclusive talents and passions have been refined over the years by the skills and experiences you acquired along the way.

You have so much to offer to the world. People are looking for your exact uniqueness in the marketplace, but they may never find it. Why? Most people have buried their authentic selves off market, invisible to all.

Frequently, people don't even value who they are. Maybe you can relate to this. Early in my career, I wrote three books on caring for older adults. One of the books was designated as a top book of the year in the field of aging by the National Library Association. In addition, by that time, I had written a number of consumer booklets that were circulating across the country.

Yet, when people asked me what I did professionally, I could not say, "I'm a writer." I did not identify with being a writer for a number of reasons. I am terrible with grammar. I don't write creatively with beautiful adjectives and adverbs that paint pictures in your mind. I have a mild case of dyslexia. I made Cs in college English.

Do you see the problem here? I was focusing on my short-comings and failed to realize that non-fiction writing is different. I failed to give myself credit for being able to organize information in a digestible format. I didn't understand at the time that editors are people who can fix the grammar and sentence structure.

Or, maybe you can relate to this. When I was trying to learn how to make money online, I looked at the gurus and I tried to copy their authenticity. I was determined to find something so I could stop trading time for dollars. But, trying to be someone else never works.

One time, a friend told me about how much money she was making with her side hustle, reselling used items on eBay. She was selling everything – clothes, shoes, electronics, and boots. One time she purchased a set of dishes in Maryland for about $40. Within 24 hours, she sold them for over $200 to a man from Pennsylvania. She had no shipping expenses because he was willing to pick them up so they would not break. She was rolling.

She told me how easy it was and gave me instructions. Despite the fact that I don't like to shop, I ran out to the same thrift store a few times a week, for a couple weeks. I purchased about 20 pairs of shoes because shoes were my friend's top sellers. I took great pictures and posted them on eBay using the best enticing descriptions I could imagine.

No bids. A few weeks later, out of frustration, I tried selling them at a garage sale. Only one pair of shoes sold.

The problem was that I was not being my authentic self and it showed up in the types and brands of shoes I had purchased. Selling was easy for my girlfriend because she is a fashionista. I am not. I purchased name brands that were a little dated and styles that probably were no longer popular.

Authenticity is what you want to bring to the market. Anything less and you might enjoy a measure of success but you may find it hard labor. Come back to your true design.

You may be thinking like the workers in the industrial age, "I don't know enough to make it on my own." That simply is not true. You will hear me time and time again say, "You can't live 45 plus years without having something to offer in the marketplace." It's never too late. Just ask these mavericks:

- Clara Pellar became a famous actress in her later years by proclaiming, "Where's the beef?" for Wendy's.
- Julia Childs wrote her first cookbook at age 50.
- Takichiro Mori left academia at age 55 and soon presided over the Japanese real estate boom.
- Harry Bernstein produced his first bestselling book at age 96 after countless rejected manuscripts.
- Henry Ford invented the Model T when he was 50 years old.
- Colonel Sanders, Harland Sanders, was 62 when he franchised Kentucky Fried Chicken after he figured out he could not live off his social security check.

Your early dreams, gifts and talents hold a clue. They may have been latent for decades, but they are still valid. In Chapter 7, you will explore more fully, aspects of the true you and possibilities in the marketplace.

You are an original. You have distinct eyes, fingerprints, hair, gifts and talents. You are the designer's innovation existing on the planet right now to contribute something that no one else can offer exactly the way you do. If you are not living this truth, it's time to take your do-over shot.

I have been told that agents who investigate counterfeit money operations learn by examining legal currency. They strive to know everything about authentic dollar bills – color, texture, print size, symbols, etc. This way, they can quickly detect any variations.

Let's take a quick look at the original you.

For the next 10 minutes, ponder the following questions. Get a pad and pen, or use your memo app to jot down your initial thoughts. Don't try to analyze them, just capture them without judgment.

- Think back to your earliest dream of success. What did it look like?
- What compliments did you frequently receive?
- What activities have you always loved?
- What were you naturally good at?
- What accomplishment have you longed to achieve your entire life?
- What makes your heart sing?

I encourage you to go back to this list and spend some time thinking about each of your responses. No, it's not just childhood foolish thinking. I call these opportunity seeds. Within these early desires and abilities lie uncharted opportunities to make money today. In the next chapter you will explore how you can effectively use these seeds.

Identity Theft

Identity theft is a real serious crime. There is a whole industry that has evolved to help you avoid being a victim. Typically, you think of an identity thief as someone who goes dumpster diving, calls you on the telephone to gain personal information or hacks into a computer system where your personal data is stored. These criminals get smarter by the day.

Interestingly, there is a category of thieves who are rarely caught and never prosecuted. These are the people who steal the truth of who you were made to be before you have an honest chance to pursue your dreams. Their weapon of choice is words. I'm sure you have heard people say:

- You aren't that good at _____
- Nobody will hire you for _____
- You can't make money by _____
- Face reality, _____ will never happen
- _____ is a foolish thing to do

Words like these are just as deadly as bullets. Limiting speech causes you to toss the opportunity seeds away, sometimes never to be found again. They hinder your ability to live out who you are truly meant to be, especially when they are said by loved ones or people in authority over you.

Once these weapons of mass destruction dwell in your heart, other thieves show up to assist them. One circumstance that doesn't unfold exactly as you had hoped becomes a caution sign; another "negative" instance creates a stop sign in your mind. You become convinced over time that you simply can't do it or become whatever your "it" is. If you agree with words that limit, your identity is stolen, and you settle for far less than your "it."

Don't get me wrong, settling for less doesn't always look bad but it simply is not fulfilling. Take Connie, for example, she always wanted to write songs and become a successful recording star. But during her young life, she frequently heard, "You can't make a decent living by singing. You are not that good."

She started smoking cigarettes, destroying her gift and never even attempted to live her dream. Connie recently retired from an OK job making OK money. In the back of her mind however, that early desire still nags, "Could I have done something with my voice."

Unfortunately, given the damage she has done to her voice over the years, it may be too late for her to sing solo, but she may be able to use her talents in other ways that bring fulfillment and remuneration. It's not too late. Connie can explore sites like www.sonicbids.com; www.reverbnation.com; or www.gigfinder.com. Maybe she can write jingles or songs or sing back up.

What about you? Early in life, you may have conformed to who you were expected to be by family and friends. Your parents may have told you something like, "There are plenty of jobs in XYZ career field," or "Government jobs provide security."

Some people chased after the almighty dollar; oftentimes, suppressing their real passions because they thought it was impossible to monetize them. You may have the good corporate job or your secure government job and you look forward to the gold watch at retirement. That's great as long as this is what you want and you are not just an actor in someone else's movie.

There is inherently nothing wrong with choosing this life path. It is only a problem when you find yourself laid off or laid up in the hospital due to stress-related illnesses. It's only a concern if you wake up in the morning and dread going to work.

Did you lock away what makes you unique and trade it for what made you successful, prestigious and popular? If so, you may have entered mid-life unsatisfied and hollow.

It's time for you to discover your own fairytale.

When you start to re-examine your opportunity seeds and combine them with the lessons and skills gained across time, something amazing happens. When you combine your genius with the unlimited prospects presented through the internet, making money becomes fun and easier than you could have ever imagined.

CHAPTER 3

Gig Economy Basics

Here's what you have been waiting for. The ONE WAY to make money online covered by this book is by using existing gig websites.

This ONE WAY requires no website, domain name, payment system or expensive equipment. In many cases, your start-up costs are nothing or very minimal. By listing current job opportunities, gig websites allow you to earn income quickly and without a lot of hassle.

I know you are wondering "What's the big secret?" I delayed this announcement because I wanted to present the foundation first. Understanding the issues that impact your ability to earn income in mid-life is important. If you are unemployed or under-employed, you now understand that many factors beyond your control are converging.

What this book is teaching is counterintuitive for most. The average person age 45 and older has been conditioned to get a full-time job, period. That's why I thought it might be helpful to introduce the concept of gig work after some context had been established.

You might be thinking, "Well, Angela, I don't know anything about this." Or you may be saying, "I'm not a digital native, I grew up with encyclopedias." No worries; you don't have to be left behind. When I discovered this simple, ONE WAY to participate in the gig economy, I was so surprised at how level the playing field has become.

This chapter provides additional evidence as to why using online gig websites is the simplest, quickest, most affordable way to earn income online. It summarizes the global gig economy – what it is and where it is headed. More importantly, you will read about how this shift in the economy will continue to impact you.

What is the Gig Economy?

How one earns income today is rapidly changing. Concepts like the "shared economy" and "gig economy" didn't even exist when you were younger. Furthermore, these terms don't even have agreed-upon definitions. Yet, every day people of all ages are making money independently by sharing and solving problems on-demand.

Let's start at the beginning. Gig work, a term borrowed from the music industry, refers to work that is temporary, part-time, intermittent, project-based, or seasonal. Sometimes it is called consulting, freelancing or contingency work. However, gig jobs are not necessarily short. I once worked a gig, part time, for almost seven years.

The gig economy refers to how companies are hiring more and more independent contractors and freelancers. Increasingly, workers are relying upon temporary, on-demand jobs. In fact, 35% of Americans are doing so.[1]

The concept of gig work is not new in the US. Back in 1946, Russell Kelly started a company to help customers with typing assignments by picking up the work and completing it at his office. Soon, companies started asking if he could send the typists to their office instead. He quickly changed his business model and name. Kelly

Girls became the first nation-wide temp agency providing temporary secretarial support in client's offices.[2]

Temporary jobs have been acceptable employment for over 70 years. However, today the structure has changed. In the early days, Kelly Girls and Manpower workers were employees of the staffing companies. Today, this is still true for some but many more workers are operating as independent workers. The gig workforce has expanded beyond office work to professional workers and experts.

The need for a temporary workforce is expanding given employees' desire for more flexibility and employers' need to cut labor costs. In fact, by the year 2020, over 43 percent of the workforce will be gig workers.[3] That's over seven million workers! This phenomenon is here to stay.

Just look at one of the largest US companies, Apple. According to a recent article in Newsweek, "Apple directly employs fewer than 10 percent of the 1 million workers who design, make and sell iMacs and iPhones."[4]

About 44 percent of business leaders realize that the changing nature of work is a top concern in industry.[5] Big businesses increasingly are hiring gig workers. In fact, the Global Contingent Workforce Study found that 20 percent of companies with more than 1,000 employees filled 30 percent of their positions with gig workers. In addition, 63 percent of corporate executives would enter the gig economy if they had the opportunity.[6]

Digital Gig Websites

I recommend that you start doing the hustle by using online gig websites to take a lot of the hassle out of finding active jobs. When you use these websites, you connect with buyers quickly. In addition, most of the heavy lifting is completed by the website company. Therefore, your main focus is doing what you already know well.

Each website works a little differently but basically they list jobs and some sites match you with opportunities based on your skill set. You also can market directly to the buyers. In other words, gig websites give you access to literally thousands, if not tens of thousands, of potential customers who are ready to buy right now. Your role is to present your abilities so they choose you to complete the work – simple.

With most sites, you don't have to bother with all of the technical stuff like curating the jobs, advertising your skills, or collecting payments from your customers. Once you have completed a job to the satisfaction of the buyer, your earnings, minus the website fees, if any, are sent to you. You don't have to wait for 30 days or more to receive payment.

I recommend using online gig sites to make money online if you want to:

- Earn income while you look for a job. Your hustle does not interfere with your job search.
- Position yourself to make money quickly. Getting started on gig websites can be done in a few hours. But I cannot ensure that someone will buy your services right way.
- Minimize your start-up costs. Many gig sites don't charge you until you make money first.
- Test a business concept. Gig sites allow you to inexpensively test the market interest in a service you are considering.

- Maintain a flexible lifestyle. You control when and where you work.
- Dust off a life-long passion and dream. Gig work can be a safe way to express talents and skills outside of your daily work responsibilities.
- Avoid in-person marketing. Gig sites allow you to sell without seeing "the whites of their eyes."

Gig websites can open up a whole new world of possibilities for you. You can use them to switch professions, test whether you can sell your passion, turn a hobby into a business, leave that oppressive job situation, earn part-time money and create freedom in your life to work when you want to and how you want. Many people use these resources to build a lucrative business by capturing the online and offline market.

The Dark Side of Gig Work

You also must understand the dark side of gig work. This is not a hustle-free situation. Some new responsibilities have to be considered. Whether you gig for the short-term or make hustling your primary source of income, keep the following in mind:

- Unpredictable earnings – Most likely, your earnings every week will be erratic.
- Lack of employee benefits – You may need to purchase your own benefits which can be expensive as you grow older, especially health insurance.
- Broader competitor base – Often, you will compete with international workers who can charge lower rates.

- Challenge of earning full-time income – You may not be able to replace your current or past income. How much you make depends on the market, your competition and your consistency.
- Potential for decreased retirement benefits – You are responsible for setting up your own retirement plans. You will not enjoy the benefit of employer matching contributions.
- Accepting low rates – Some gig clients pay very low. Consider how much time and energy a job will take to ensure you receive a fair rate.
- Change in gig site policies – Gig sites can change their policies at any time. For example, if they increase their transaction fees, you may receive less for the work performed.
- Responsibilities that come with operating a business - You are required to pay quarterly income taxes, for example. There may be other legal requirements necessary for the establishment of a business. This information is covered in Chapter 5.

I encourage you, embrace the digital marketplace immediately. Use existing website platforms to find buyers who are ready to purchase your unique gifts, talents and skills. Access the international audience from the comfort of your own computer or cell phone screen. Set your own hours and place of work. Remember, you are the product. This is an exciting era!

References

1   Intuit. "Intuit: Gig economy is 34% of US workforce." CNNMoney. Accessed February 05, 2018. http://money.cnn.com/2017/05/24/ news/economy/gig-economy-intuit/index.html.

2   Kelly Girl Story | Kelly Services. Accessed February 05, 2018. https://www.kellyservices.us/us/about-us/company-informa- tion/kelly-girl-story/.

3   Intuit. "Intuit: Gig economy is 34% of US workforce." CNNMoney. Accessed February 05, 2018. http://money.cnn.com/2017/05/24/ news/economy/gig-economy-intuit/index.html.

4   Reich, Robert. "The Downside of the Gig Economy." Newsweek. April 15, 2016. Accessed February 05, 2018. http://www.news- week.com/downside-gig-economy-365422.

5   The Future of Jobs. Accessed February 05, 2018. http://www3. weforum.org/docs/WEF_Future_of_Jobs.pdf

6   Mavenlink. "New Research: 4 On-Demand Workforce Trends." The White-Collar Gig Economy Four Workforce Trends. Ac- cessed February 05, 2018. http://go.mavenlink.com/the-white- collar-gig-economy-four-workforce-trends.

CHAPTER 4

Renewing Your Mind:
As You Think, So You Are

Although the global digital marketplace is open to all, many people age 45 and older, will never enter into it. Most don't even know that the marketplace exists. Many will never explore the digital gig marketplace because it is unfamiliar territory.

You may be wondering, "Is this marketplace too dangerous, too mysterious, too difficult to master and only for the young?" No, it is not.

Like any marketplace, you need to watch your digital purse. You won't enter your credit card number on the counter of a website that looks shady. Like any other market, you shop until you find the store, the website, where you want to do business. As you shop, just like in the mall, you will find lots of young people there, but generally people of all ages are out shopping.

Contrary to popular belief, however, the complexity of the digital marketplace is not the barrier for people 45-plus. What will keep people who are reading this book from doing well by using online gig websites is not a lack of knowledge or money or time; it is their mindset. Their fingers can't enter where their minds refuse to go. They need a mindset re-set. It is the first step.

If you have not worked in the digital gig space before, you will want to examine and evaluate your beliefs. You may have to abandon thoughts that are not serving you well and entertain new ideas about technology, your abilities and your earning potential.

The world around us is changing. Change will not wait for anyone to believe it or embrace it. Although the traditional approaches to work are still with us, they are fading fast. Just as we are headed for a paperless, cashless society, we are also approaching a time when work and the workplace will look very different. It's time to prepare.

This chapter explores the limiting mindset that keeps people lost behind the outside walls of success. You will focus on possibility thinking and learn a proven tactic for opening your mind to embrace transformation. By the end the chapter, you may want to reexamine the opportunity seeds you uncovered in the previous chapter. If you cultivate them with a new mindset, maybe the seeds will grow.

Understanding Mindset and Transformation

Before we talk about transforming your mindset, let's unpack what a mindset really is. According to dictionary. com, mindset is an attitude, disposition, or mood. It is also described as an intention or inclination.

According to noted psychologist from Standard University, Dr. Carol Dweck, there are fixed mindsets and growth mindsets. People with a fixed mindset believe that some people have the necessary success traits like talents and intelligence while others simply don't. They tend to give little importance to effort. The fixed mindset negatively judges every challenge and set back. This type of thinking keeps you bound in fear and doubt.[1]

People with a growth mindset, on the other hand, believe that through initiative and hard work, they can develop their abilities. They are resilient, love learning and tend to persevere to accomplish great things. They take positive actions to improve and thrive during the most challenging situations. This is possibility thinking.

Understanding mindset leads us to a discussion of the issue, what is transformation? According to dictionary.com, transformation is a change in form, appearance, nature, or character. When you transform your mindset, you change your life completely.

I love the way Dean Anderson and Linda Ackerman Anderson describe transformation in *Change Leaders' Network*[2]. They are talking about organizational development but there are some important lessons to be learned when people incorporate change in their lives.

The Andersons refer to the simplest type of change as developmental change. This is when you improve how you currently do something but you don't change what you do.

Transitional change replaces what you currently are doing with something completely new. It means you must emotionally let go of the old way of doing things. Typically, in transitional change, you know where you are headed so you can manage the transition. However, this type of change does not require a radical shift in culture or behavior.

Transformation is a totally different animal. It's more amorphous. The "what" and the "how" may not be clear. It involves an unknown future state and includes a good deal of trial and error. The required change emerges and you must operate in the unknown which is frightening for most people. We prefer the comfort of the familiar.

As transformation happens, it requires different mindsets, behaviors, and perspectives because everything becomes radically different. The Andersons help us see that true transformation is complicated and takes time. That is why coaches who guarantee transformation when they have never even experienced it and don't understand it are frustrating.

Mindset and Money Making On Your Own

How does all of this relate to your making money online? Good question.

First, if you have been working for someone else your whole life, then you probably think and act like an employee. Maybe receiving a predictable pay check every two weeks is comforting. You have a routine. You go to the same place every day, work with the same people, and sit at the same desk.

To earn income on your own, however, involves a tremendous transformation, especially if you decide to go after a different line of work. Your work setting will be different and your work might vary. No one is going to motivate you to meet your metrics. You may need to learn some new skills quickly to complement what you already know. You might have to work alone at times.

The road to making money online probably won't go the way you expect. No major change in life ever does. You may not really know what to expect. Sure this book provides tips and tools for a simple affordable way to approach online business. Nonetheless, you will have to approach this transition or transformation with an open mind.

If you have a growth mindset, although you may not have experience yet, you are ready to learn and you know you can do this with a little guidance. It won't matter if you aren't a natural salesman or you are not totally comfortable with computers. These are things you can learn. You might be afraid of the unknown, but just keep moving forward. This resource will guide you.

If your mindset is fixed, you can come up with a thousand excuses about why hustling on gig websites won't work for you. You will be afraid to try. Maybe you are fearful that there is too much to learn or that you might be unsuccessful. Remember what Henry Ford said: "Failure is simply the opportunity to begin again, this time more intelligently." (www.brainyquote.com)[3].

You might say, "I just don't know what to do." Don't worry about it. You will learn. Remember, true transformation is scary, unknown but exhilarating and profitable at the same time.

Open your eyes to the possibilities. There truly is a way to earn income outside of traditional means. You have something wonderful that others find valuable and are willing to purchase. With your years of experience, practice and life, you already have 70 to 90 percent of what you need. You truly have a mid-life opportunity in front of you; not a mid-life crisis.

If you need to change your mindset, try the process that follows. Although these steps are simple, they are not easy. For some, your current thought patterns may be like the old records we used to play. No matter where you drop the needle, you end up in the same old groove until the music ends.

Some of you may have tried making money on your own but it didn't work out the way you anticipated. So what? Think about Thomas Edison. He conducted over 9,000 experiments when inventing the alkaline storage battery. A colleague of his reported:

This [the research] had been going on more than five months, seven days a week, when I was called down to the laboratory to see him. 'Isn't it a shame that with the tremendous amount of work you have done you haven't been able to get any results?' I said. Edison turned like a flash, and with a smile replied: *'Results! Why, man, I have gotten lots of results! I know several thousand things that won't work!'* (*http://edison.rutgers. edu/newsletter9.html*)[4].

Changing Your Mindset

Ready to be transformed? Here are the four simple steps offered by Dr. Carol Dweck for changing a fixed mindset to a more positive mindset[5]:

1. Listen to your thoughts. Unchecked thoughts lead to repetitive thinking and enter into your heart as a belief. The Bible states, and many philosophers agree: you become what you think in your heart. Being aware of your thought life is important.
2. Know that you can choose which mindset approach to entertain. You are not limited to reacting and thinking the way you always have.

3. Talk back with a growth mindset perspective. The chart below provides some very common thought patterns that you can choose from.

Fixed Mindset Limited Thinking	Growth Mindset Possibility Thinking
I have tried this before and failed.	Let me see what I can do differently than what I did the first time. Most successful people fail a few times.
I don't know anything about all of this online stuff.	I will find a book to learn about online stuff. I will also ask _____ to help me.
I don't have any money to waste.	People say you can begin a business with very little money. I can find out how.
I don't have any skills to offer online.	Surely there is something I can offer online.
I don't want to spend all of my free time trying to figure out how to do things online.	I will start with one hour a day to explore my options.
I can't.	I will.

4. Take the action that results from the growth mindset. Dr. Dweck suggests that you take the action that challenges you and helps you learn from setbacks. Listen and learn from criticism and act on it if appropriate.

A final thought on mindset. This quote is taken from a book written in 1951 by William Hutchinson Murray called *The Scottish Himalayan Expedition*[6].

"Until one is committed, there is hesitancy, the chance to draw back. Concerning all acts of initiative (and creation), there is one elementary truth, the ignorance of which kills countless ideas and splendid plans: that the moment one definitely commits oneself, then Providence moves too. All sorts of things occur to help one that would never otherwise have occurred. A whole stream of events issues from the decision, raising in one's favor all manner of unforeseen incidents and meetings and material assistance, which no man could have dreamed would have come his way. Whatever you can do, or dream you can do, begin it. Boldness has genius, power, and magic in it. Begin it now."

References

[1] "MINDSET." Mindset | What is Mindset. Accessed February 05, 2018. https://www.mindsetonline.com/whatisit/about/index.html.

[2] Change Leaders' Network http://changeleadersnetwork.com/free-resources/what-is-transformation-and-why-is-it-so-hard-to-manage.

[3] "Henry Ford Quotes." BrainyQuote. Accessed February 05, 2018. https://www.brainyquote.com/authors/henry_ford.

[4] Quote Investigator. Accessed February 05, 2018. https://quoteinvestigator.com/2012/07/31/edison-lot-results/.

[5] "MINDSET." Mindset | What is Mindset. Accessed February 05, 2018. https://www.mindsetonline.com/whatisit/about/index.html.

[6] "A quote by William Hutchison Murray." Quote by William Hutchison Murray: "Until one is committed, there is hesitancy, the...". Accessed February 05, 2018. https://www.goodreads.com/quotes/128689-until-one-is-committed-there-is-hesitancy-the-chance-to.

Part II: Primed

Prepare (someone) for a situation or task, typically by supplying them with relevant information. (dictionary.com)

CHAPTER 5

The Business Side of Profit

When you earn income using digital gig sites to find work, you might be engaging in business activities. (I say "might" because some gig workers are hired as employees of companies that send them out on gigs.) The Internal Revenue Service (IRS) states that "an activity qualifies as a business if it is carried on with the reasonable expectation of earning a profit." Sometimes gig workers forget this. But you shouldn't.

This chapter discusses the business of online gig work. Some of the issues highlighted in this chapter may not apply to you. Each situation is different and depends on what type of business you want to start. In *The Five Faces of the On-demand Economy,* Intuit delineates five approaches to gig work[1].

1. Substituters – people who replace the income of a traditional job that is no longer available.
2. Passionistas – those looking for a way to express their passion for profit.
3. Side Giggers – people supplementing their income to create financial stability.
4. Career Freelancer – anyone building a career through independent work.

5. Business Builders – people driven by the desire to be the boss.

After deciding where you see yourself on this list, you can structure your gig work and be their own boss.

This chapter does not provide legal advice. It presents an overview of the most common steps to form a business. You are strongly encouraged to consult legal and tax professionals within your state and county for specific local requirements.

Why Do I Have to Start a Business?

"Business is generally defined as "the activity of making, buying, or selling goods or providing services in exchange for money." Working gig assignments is conducting business.

Keep in mind, however, you don't need to have a "formal company structure" to make money on gig websites. You can work under your own name as an independent contractor using only your social security number. Most online giggers are self-employed and work alone.

The following steps are offered for your consideration. If you are going to become a full-time gig worker, many of these steps might apply to you.

Business Name

You don't need a company name to succeed in the online gig economy, you can work under you own name and use your personal bank account and social security number. However, you may want to select one to make it easier to keep your personal finances separate from the business.

Deciding on a company name is important. Experts suggest finding a name that creates a specific brand image. For example, Jessica's Perfect Transcripts or Affordable IT Solutions are names that tell you the exact services being offered.

The bottom line is making sure you can legally use the name you prefer; it resonates with customers and it is a name you can stick to for years to come. Consider the following steps before officially registering your company name with your state:

- Search the internet to see if someone is already using your name. Play around with the name you like by adding a word before or after it in order to find one that is not already in use.
- Search a domain name registrar such as GoDaddy (www.godaddy.com) or Host Gator (www.hostgator.com) to find a domain name you can purchase as your online business name. A domain name is the address people use when they search for you on the internet. It is the words that come after the "www."
- Find the agency within your state that registers trade names. A trade name may cost $10 - $50 to register and gives you legal permission to use that name for business within a state.
- If your goal is to establish a large national corporation or you want the ultimate protection over your name, you may want to consider establishing a trademark for your business name so no one else can use it for the type of business you estab-

lish. Visit the US Patent and Trademark website for more information (https://www.uspto.gov/). Be aware, that trade marking a name is time consuming and expensive. Large brand names like Pepsi, Lexus, IBM, etc., usually are trademarked. Again, most people hustling through online gig sites do not apply for a trade mark.

Legal Structure

You will need to select a legal structure for your business. Your legal structure determines what tax forms you file, what you assume personal responsibility for and how potential funders view your operation. Consult a tax or business expert for more details.

There are several ways to structure a business. Following are a few considerations for each of the structures you will consider[2]:

- Sole proprietor – This is the simplest structure used for individual ownership of an unincorporated business. You use your own social security number for tax purposes. You are personally responsible for the company's liabilities.
- Partnerships – This structure allows more than one person to own the business. In a general partnership all partners manage the company, share the profits, and have joint liability for the debts of the partnership. A limited liability partnership excludes limited partners from the liabilities of the partnership.
- LLC – a Limited Liability Company limits the personal liability of owners and allows earnings to be

taxed on either the owner's personal taxes or at the corporate level.

- Corporations – Corporate structures are much more complex and expensive to maintain. However, corporations are considered separate legal entities and thereby shield owners from personal liability. Corporations also have more potential tax write offs. This is the structure most likely to secure investments.
- S Corporation - Most small business owners choose a special class of corporation called an S Corporation that allows pass-through taxation. This means no income taxes are paid at the business level. Business profit or loss is passed-through to the owners' personal tax returns. Any necessary tax is reported and paid at the individual level.

EIN (Employer Identification Number)

In most cases, you may want to register for an EIN with the IRS. However, if you are a sole proprietor or LLC without employees and do not file pension or excise tax returns, you are not required to have an EIN. Think of this number as your company's social security number. You will use it to open your business bank account, register with the state and pay your federal taxes. You can complete the application online FREE at www.irs.gov.

Business Plan

Depending on your goals, you may or may not want to complete a business plan. A business plan is a way to capture your goals, research, plans and projections for your business. Many people who hustle using gig websites never develop a business plan. They basically just keep looking for and bidding on jobs, learning to tweak their bids better and better and simply make as much money as they can.

Those who are dedicated to growing their revenue steadily, building a team to get the work done, and establishing a recognizable brand may want to complete a business plan. It is absolutely necessary if you want to attract traditional funding from a bank or investors to start and grow a business.

A business plan should be dynamic; it should grow and evolve, and evolve as you learn and develop. It is a tool you can use to stay on focus and plot your way to success. It should be something you refer to often.

Today, however, many people who work solo, without staff, or with partners, avoid traditional business plans like a plague. They are too long, take too much time to complete, and often end up on the top of a book shelf collecting dust, never to be referred to again.

Personally, I like a simple business plan. One that gets your thoughts churning and decisions made about what your business will really become and how it will operate. A copy of one tool you might want to use is presented on page 47. This *Fizzle Business Sketch Template with Questions*[3] is provided by an organization called Fizzle that offers business training. You can get a FREE blank copy of this wonderful tool at https://fizzle.co.

Again, most online gig workers do not write a business plan. However, creating one might be helpful especially if you want to expand, hire workers or combine the online gig work with offline activities. If you follow it, the plan keeps you on track to move towards your business goals.

THE FIZZLE BUSINESS SKETCH TEMPLATE WITH QUESTIONS

PROBLEM	ELEVATOR PITCH	SOLUTION
What problem(s) are you solving? What desire(s) are you satisfying?	In one powerful sentence combine your problem, audience, solution and differentiator. (maybe try a few variations)	How will you solve this problem? What's valuable about it to your audience?

AUDIENCE	CHANNELS	KEY METRICS	DIFFERENTIATOR	REVENUE
Who do you serve? Who are your most important customers? What are their defining qualities?	How does this audience want to be reached? Where are they already? How will they find you?	What will you measure to determine that THIS audience has THIS problem and wants THIS solution?	What is different/unique about your solution?	What will you sell to them? How much will it cost?

COSTS	BUSINESS BOOSTERS	PERSONAL FIT
What costs and activities will you need to build this business? (hosting, advertising, development, etc) What do you need to make this business happen outside of yourself?	What unfair advantages do you have over the competition? (relationships, access, experience, etc) How is your solution not easily copied?	Does this business feel like you? Is this the kind of customer/lifestyle/responsibility you want? Will you get tired of this or does it energize you to think about it?

Taxes

Once you make your first dime using digital gig sites, you are officially in business according to the IRS. Uncle Sam wants his portion of all that you earn and expects you to report every nickel. If you earn $400 profit or more, you are required to file a Schedule C tax return to show your business income and expenses. However, if you earn less than $600 from any one source, your client is not obligated to report it to the IRS, although they may. You want to accurately report all income.

Under certain circumstances, gig websites will send the IRS and you a 1099K (record of payments made) if they paid you directly and you made over $20,000 with more than 200 transactions[4]. The good news is you can deduct some of your business expenses on your taxes such as refunds, fees, WIFI costs, cost of a computer, etc.

Whether you want to work a few hours per week or full time, the IRS expects you to make quarterly tax payments on income earned to avoid fines. The only way to get out of this is to make sure you owe less than $1,000 at tax time. (As the tax laws are in flex as you read, check with a tax professional for updates.)

Also, consult with your state taxation office as every state handles internet sales taxation differently. Today, states cannot require internet businesses, with no physical presence within a state, to pay that state's income tax. However, as internet sales continue to grow, more and more states will seek to have this law abolished. Stay tuned.

Licenses and Insurance

Your state's licensing and permits office will help you determine if you need a professional, business or occupational license. The same applies to liability insurance. In most cases, you will only need these if your profession requires them.

Some jurisdictions may require a general business license or a home business permit. If you live in a condominium or other controlled association, you may want to check with your home owners association to be sure your business meets their requirements for conducting your business at home.

In concluding this chapter, I want to remind you of two things: First, most people using online gig sites make money without much hassle. They don't establish a company structure. They work under their own names, use their own social security numbers, and do not hire employees. Even so, they must still abide by the applicable Federal and state laws

Second, this chapter is just an overview of what you need to know. Consult professionals to help you make these critical decisions.

References

[1] Intuit. *"The Five Faces of the On-Demand Economy"* Investors.intuit.com. (2018). The Five Faces of the On-Demand Economy. Accessed 5 Feb. 2018, http://investors.intuit.com/Press-Releases/Press-Release-Details/2016/The-Five-Faces-of-the-On-Demand-Economy/default.aspx.

[2] SBA. "Choose Your Business Structure." *The U.S. Small Business Administration | SBA.gov.* Accessed February 05, 2018. Available at: https://www.sba.gov/starting-business/choose-your-business-structure/.

[3] The Fizzle Business Sketch with Questions https://fizzle.co.

[4] TurboTax. "What Online Business Owners Should Know about IRS Form 1099-K
TurboTax; Taxes, I. (2018). Accessed 5 Feb. 2018. https://turbotax.intuit.com/tax-tips/small-business-taxes/what-online-business-owners-should-know-about-irs-form-1099-k/L2tODOz3r.

CHAPTER 6

A Short Chapter: Tools You Will Need

Do you know why this is a short chapter? It's short because to do the hustle as described in this book means a lot less hassle! Certainly, there are some basic tools you will need. **No, you don't have to cash out your retirement fund** to make it happen but you may have to spend some money.

This chapter reviews the basic tools you will need to use online gig sites. I promise you, you will be amazed at how little you really need to get started. Some of these tools you can borrow if you don't already have them or can't afford to buy them right now.

Computer

You definitely need access to a computer. If you do not own one, you can borrow a computer, rent one or use computers available at the public library.

Be aware that not having a computer may limit when you can work, but not necessarily. Many of the gig sites have smartphone apps you can use to run your business.

If you use a public computer, you run the risk of being hacked. That means the bad guys can break into your accounts to steal and destroy. If you leave your passwords and user names on a shared computer, someone also may gain access to your personal data.

So, if you can't afford a computer initially, your goal should be to purchase one as soon as possible. Buy the best computer you can afford. Go to a few computer stores, talk with the salesperson about your money making venture; how you plan to expand and let them suggest some options. Once you know what you require, you can go bargain shopping.

Here's a tip: Research the best price for the computer you want. If possible, take less cash to the store than the best price you could find. Count the money in front of the sales person and say "This is all I have; what can you do for me?" If they can't lower the price, ask for free software or extended warranty. When I tried this, I saved $200 on my computer and received free antivirus software.

Internet Service

It would be pretty hard to work online if you can't get online, (unless you work on your cell phone). Find an internet provider that offers high speed services at the least expensive price. Today you can easily find a provider for about $30 to $40 per month. Or, you can have the internet bundled with other services like telephone and cable television for a discount. Contact local internet providers for more information.

Software

Select the software you need based on what you offer online. In many cases, but not all, it might be helpful to have Microsoft Office software (Word, Excel, Outlook, PowerPoint, etc.). You can download Adobe Acrobat Reader, free software that allows you to read PDF files.

PDF (portable document format) ensures that files look the same when viewed on different computer systems or when printed on different printers. Research what software is commonly used by people selling a similar service.

Email Address

An email address, or online mailbox, is typically part of the online gig communication system. Most websites will require you to provide your email address when you register. Although gig websites usually have an internal mailbox system for communicating with your customers, they typically send you alerts by regular email.

There are a number of free email providers such as Gmail, Yahoo, Zoho, iCloud, Hotmail and many more. If you want to personalize your email address, you will need to purchase a domain name also. A domain name is basically an online address. It's the name whereby people access your website. For example, here's the pattern for a domain name, www. (yourdomainname).com.

Payment System

An e-payment system is a way to process payments online electronically. Depending on the website platforms you work on, you may be able to use your credit card, PayPal, your bank account, wire transfer or other payment methods to get paid. Check with the platforms you intend to work on to set up a payment system that works for you.

Remember, when selecting which platform to use, be sure to understand the various fees you will be responsible for and how payment is made. Many platforms are free to join so you don't spend any money until you make money. Some, however, charge a registration fee or monthly membership fees. Others have fees associated with extra promotion. You should factor fees into your pricing.

Most gig websites operate by receiving the payment from the customer; taking out their fees and then depositing the balance into your account. To take funds out of your account, you need to transfer them to your bank account or credit card.

Other Tools

Depending on what you do to earn money, you may have other important resources to purchase. For example, if you are editing video, you will need video editing software and a computer with lots of memory to handle the work. Writers might purchase grammar software. If you have so many clients that it's challenging to keep up with them, a tracking app for freelancers might be helpful.

The bottom line is to know what you need and purchase the tools that you can afford. Look for free resources first, borrow, or barter next. Once you make more money, you can upgrade.

CHAPTER 7

You Already Know Enough

As I travel around the country speaking, one thing I constantly advise, "You can't live 45-plus years and not have something to offer for profit. It's simply impossible." Yet often people assert, "I am a generalist. I'm not great at anything in particular." Or, they may say, "I know what I love to do, but no one will pay me to do it."

I repeat, you can't live 45-plus years and not have something to offer for profit. I can help you figure it out. I challenge anyone to prove me wrong.

In this chapter, you are going to examine what you already know and what you can already do. Start by exploring your "why." If you have a compelling, motivating reason why you want to undertake new money-making opportunities, you will find them and be successful.

Next, you will complete the GIG Worksheet (Generate Ideas for Gigging) to uncover your online possibilities. You will end this chapter having identified categories of gig websites that you want to explore.

Some of you may be tempted to skip this worksheet because you believe you already know the types of jobs you want to pursue online. However, you might identify other options by using the GIG worksheet. You can use this worksheet to identify potential new careers, turn a hobby into a business or use skills you have forgotten about.

Your Why

In *Start with Why: How Great Leaders Inspire Everyone to Take Action*[1], Simon Sinek explains that a clearly expressed "why" separates you from others. Ask yourself, why you want to make extra money; why do you want to work in your chosen field? By starting with your "why" you position yourself to focus and persevere.

You can have two complementary "whys." Your first why is altruistic and higher than your need for making money. It's unselfish. It is rooted in adding value to others. It has to inspire you. This extra factor causes potential clients and customers to appreciate your passion and commitment because it's genuine.

Your second compelling why is self-focused, practical and explains why you want to make more money through gig work. It is about your freedom of expression, control of your time and what you can accomplish with the additional cash.

After years of fumbling along online trying to make money in several different ways, I asked myself why am I doing this; what value am I bringing to the lives of others? I didn't enjoy what I was attempting and I was not prospering because I was not building on what I already knew and enjoyed.

Eventually, I uncovered my altruistic why. It is related to the frustration I experience when I see brilliant people stuck in unfulfilling job situations or are hopeless because they got laid off. This really bothers me because I know I can help people live more fulfilling lives. With this in mind, I took the skills and talents I already had as an entrepreneur and trainer to help people monetize their skill set through online and offline programs.

My second more practical why is rooted in my son's health challenge. I could not sustain myself using my old model of business. When I did not work, I did not get paid. After almost going bankrupt, I promised myself, never again. That's why I explored online opportunities.

What are your whys? Go ahead and write them below.

GIG (Generating Ideas for Gigging) Worksheet

Knowing the type of gig work you want to secure online may be simple for some. Others, however, may not have a clue about what to go after. If you are still searching for your possibilities or fine-tuning them, this worksheet will help you. Many have found it insightful, especially when they desired a different type of work.

The GIG Worksheet opens your eyes to where your talents, skills, passions and experience converge in the marketplace. It helps you see the numerous possibilities for making money using what you already know and like to do. Yes, you may need to learn some new comple-mentary skills, but you are already 80 percent there.

This simple worksheet allows you to examine all that you could bring to the marketplace. You will identify which of your offerings are already attractive to buyers using online gig sites. You will be amazed by the prospects.

The beauty of this process is that you take a holistic view of yourself and the marketplace, thereby, increasing your options for finding work. If you have a growth mindset, seize this opportunity to examine unfamiliar promising ways to earn income.

Part A - A 360 Degree View of You

This is a brain dumping exercise where you look at who you are in totality for maybe the first time in years. Many get stuck thinking only about themselves in terms of what they have been paid to do in recent years. But you are much more than that. (This is the same exercise I created for myself to identify my own life work.)

As you complete the list that follows, be exhaustive. Don't make any judgments about whether you can make money with a particular quality. The key is to think about how you are wired and what you're made of.

	List Your Unique Qualities Here
My Talents Include: (Innate qualities and natural aptitude like painting, fixing things, drawing)	
My Hard Skills Are: (Knowledge and abilities that have been taught or practiced like programming, speaking a foreign language, accounting)	
My Expertise Is: (Areas of great skill. These can be drawn from all of the lists above)	
Special Training and Certifications	
Hobbies: (Activities done strictly for pleasure)	
Curiosity: (List things that peak your interest. What do you want to learn more about?)	
Passion: (What arouses deep emotions in you such as a cause or a goal?)	
Physical Capacity: (Do you have a special physical ability? List it here.)	

Think back to when you were young. What were your gifts and talents? Don't forget any special certifications, life experience or classes you have taken along the way. List everything in the chart. If you run out of space, use another sheet of paper.

Now, go back through these lists once more to make sure you have captured everything you can acknowledge about yourself. Have you included gifts and skills from when you were a young child, a high school student and a young professional?

Part B - Existing Gig Opportunities

On the following page, you'll find a chart that lists categories for the types of gigs available on websites right now. In the column beside each category is a delineation of the specific types of gigs it includes. As you review Part A of this worksheet, place a checkmark next to the category of work on Part B that matches your interests. Circle the specific jobs you could pursue within the selected categories. After you conclude this exercise, you will have identified numerous gig possibilities.

Once you've completed the exercise, you will have a sense of what makes you unique and the types of jobs that are currently available. Now go back and review the categories you selected, then choose one category to test. If it's hard to choose, think about what makes your heart sing or where your true genius is found.

Gig Category	Available Gig Work (circle potential jobs)
☐ Administration	• Call center • Customer service • Data entry • Transcription • Virtual assistant • Web research
☐ Business	• Advertising • Accounting • Business consulting • Customer relationship management • E-commerce • Email marketing • Financial management • Human resources • Lead generation • Market research • Public relations • Sales • Search engine optimization • Social media management
☐ Creative	• Animation • Audio production • Graphic design • Illustration • Logo creation • Packaging • Photography • PowerPoint • Video production • Voice over
☐ General & 50-Plus	• Wide variety of jobs
☐ International	• Jobs outside the US
☐ Other	• Coaching • Testing websites and software

☐ Specialties Professions	• 3-D modeling • Architecture • Electrical engineering • Engineering • Intellectual property • Health • Legal services • Medical services
☐ Tech	• Artificial intelligence • Cyber security • Data management • Gaming • Mobile apps • Networking • Programming • Quality assurance • Software development • System administration • Website development
☐ Tutoring	• Test preparation • Children • Adults
☐ Writing	• Academic writing • Blogging • Business writing • Copywriting • Creative Writing • Editing • Proposal writing • Web content • Translation services

This is only your first test category. Remember, although it is more challenging to earn income in categories where you have little experience, it can be done. Your old dreams can become a new source of income but it might take time and ingenuity at the beginning. If you are multi-talented, you can test as many categories as you like, but only one at a time. If you need money quickly, however, start where you have the most experience.

List your test category here:

_____

List the types of jobs you want to go after in the test category:

_____

_____

_____

In this chapter, you discovered what you have to offer that the market is buying. In the next chapter, you will find out where in the digital marketplace you can thrive.

Reference

[1]   Minors, P. (2018). *Start With Why by Simon Sinek | Book Summary*. Accessed 5 Feb. 2018, https://paulminors.com/start-simon-sinek-book-summary-pdf-old.

CHAPTER 8

Which Gig Sites Work Best for You

Congratulations! You have assessed your many talents, skills and passions, and identified one category of gig websites to test. Certain websites will work well for you. They list numerous jobs for you to go after and they operate in a manner that you prefer. Other websites may not work as well. This chapter helps you to select the website that could be the most profitable for you. Then, you will test them one by one.

Examining Potential Gig Platforms

Determining the most suitable websites for you is a process. You may be tempted to just select a few and start working on them. This is inadvisable. By doing so, you dilute your focus on and mastery of any one website. Experienced online gig workers recommend that you start with one site, master it and then expand to others.

The Digital Marketplace list is found in Chapter 12. Although it is comprehensive, it is not an exhaustive list. You may find other sites that would be appropriate for your needs. Every attempt was made to list reputable sites. However, we make no guarantees about the accuracy of the information provided. Websites come and go every day and they change their policies frequently. Users are responsible for researching each site.

Go to the Digital Marketplace and locate the category you want to test. You will find a list of websites under each category. As you read through the summary of these gig websites, select three or four that you think might be best for you to find work. Take your time and examine these sites and decide which one you want to test first.

You don't want to spend a lot of time on this initial review of gig sites, but you do want to have an understanding of how they each operate before you get started using them. A few recommendations for selecting gig websites to start testing include:

- If possible, get a sense of how many gigs would be available for you. Look for the specific jobs that you circled earlier. For example, if you are a scientific writer, don't consider a website that caters to romance writers.
- Look for reviews. Check with the Better Business Bureau (www.bbb.com). Also search for "reviews" and "complaints" followed by the website's name.
- Read through the "About" and "How It Works" pages. Often these pages will provide important information to help you select the first site to test.
- Find out how long the website has been in operation. Go to www.whois.com and type in the address for the website you are examining. Generally, the longer a site has been around the more stable it tends to be. Keep in mind, however, this online gig website concept has only become popular during

the last five to seven years or so, although there are some sites that have been around much longer.

- Make sure you understand fees. Common fees include membership, transaction, and administrative charges. Fees can be charged to the gig worker, the hiring organization or both.
- Visit the FAQs (frequently asked questions), the website blog and community. These resources offer details about how the gig website operates.
- Choose which gig website you want to test first.

Conduct a Market Test

Your market test can take as long as four to six weeks. You should start getting gigs (jobs) by this time. However, if at any point you discover something that you don't like on the first gig site, move on to the next test website. If your offering does not attract buyers on a particular gig site, don't worry. Just try another one. Again, every website is not for everyone.

Your testing will consist of learning the intricacies of the gig site you selected and implementing what you learn. That means reading blog posts containing helpful tips, participating in the community, using the help feature when you don't understand something and studying the top sellers.

During your testing period, dedicate two to three hours per day learning the site and applying for jobs. People who are serious about making money may work even longer online. Putting the work in at the very beginning of your test will help you determine much faster if the site you are considering will be profitable for you.

To be successful, be pro-active about looking several times a day for jobs you want. Remember, the internet never sleeps. There is someone somewhere in the world buying and selling at all times. How long it takes to find your first job depends on a number of factors. Market demand at the time you register with a gig website, your competition and your commitment level all influence your success.

Remember that a testing period is really a test. Your consistency and flexibility are the ingredients you need to evaluate what is right for you. So don't get disappointed if you don't get as many gigs as you would like at the start. Research what works and improve your approach over time. Many gig workers had to experiment to find the right site and best way of working to succeed. So will you.

Check Out Your Competitors

An important part of testing a website is checking out how the competition is succeeding. Honestly, one of the downsides to doing the hustle using internet gig sites is that some of the buyers are looking for the lowest cost.

That's why it's critical for you to highlight your value and what differentiates you from the crowd. You will be competing against fellow gig workers from India, the Philippines and all over the world. In many countries, the cost of living is much less than ours, so they can charge far less. Conversely, many buyers, after having been dissatisfied with cheap labor, are now only interested in quality.

Checking out your competition is very important. Most of the gig sites listed in the digital marketplace, like the offline world, accept blind applications meaning you can't find out who is applying for the job and what they are saying.

If the site is primarily an aggregated listing of available flexible jobs, like www.execsearches.com, www.tempandparttimejobs.com and www.workingnomads.co, then you simply treat each job within the list the same way you do any other online job listings. Your research is focused on the company needing temporary or part-time workers and the actual job.

Some websites like www.Freelancer.com and www.LocalSolo.com allow you to gather information on people you might be bidding against. Do your research and gain insight as to how top performers prosper. Adopt their tactics that make sense for you. Learn some secrets for success by doing the following:

- Find the top sellers. Do a Google search of "top sellers on _____ (insert name of gig website)" or "success stories" or other phrases to identify who is being successful. In limited cases, you will find top sellers on the site itself. For example, www.99designs.com allows you to see all of the work of your competitors. You can then search them in Google to learn more. Sites like www.upwork.com permit you to see the actual income of your competitors. Don't forget to look at the website's blog and forum. Typically, you can quickly tell the successful users. They have a lot of advice to offer.
- If possible review their profiles and take notes. Pay close attention to what they say and how they say it. Make a list of the keywords they use and how they describe their services. You will want to use the same words to construct your profile. Look

at how they bid for jobs. In other words, learn as much as you can

- Go to your competitor's website and social media profiles if they have them. Again, make notes about how they describe themselves. Look at what their reviews and recommendations say. This will help you learn the attributes valued by buyers that you can use when describing your work, but only if it's true.
- Contact your competitors, if you feel comfortable. Let them know that you are entering the field and find out if you can collaborate with them on some projects. They may be willing to share some great advice.

Figuring out which gig websites work for you is critical for success. Remember you are just testing so you never fail. Basically, you are simply eliminating sites from your consideration if they don't work out. Also, keep in mind that once you get established on a site, you will get more gigs and can raise your rates. The next chapter is helpful as it contains tips on how to win as an online gig worker.

CHAPTER 9

Winning Tips

Every gig site operates differently. However, there are three basic types of sites; job boards, bid sites and match websites. Some gig sites combine these different approaches, thus offering more opportunities for you to find work.

Additionally, special features such as memberships, preferred status, profile reviews, and more, help increase your possibility of being found. Typically fees are associated with special features.

This chapter reviews tactics and tips for landing a gig. Implement the ideas that best meet your needs and are appropriate for the gig site you decide to use. It is important to have a clear understanding of how the gig site operates and how your competitors are getting jobs. These winning tips will help you.

Three Types of Gig Sites

The most common gig websites are job boards. Opportunities are typically searchable by industry, position, location, etc. Companies pay to list their openings or jobs are curated from various sources around the internet.

If you use a job board site, you apply for gigs online and the buyers decide if they want to hire you. You may go back and forth with the potential client asking questions and receiving clarification before you are hired. To find gig work, you may need to search using terms like – part time, temporary job, and seasonal work. Some job boards have a matching component where they suggest a short list of candidates to the hiring company.

The second type of gig websites involves bidding on work. Buyers list a project and how much they are willing to pay. You bid on the job by stating what you would charge and how you would approach the work. Often the selection of gig workers on these sites is price-driven. Sometimes the client is looking for quality at a reasonable price. Your job is to convince the potential client that you are worth your bid.

Some bid sites run contests where you bid with your work. Typically contests are for creative design work like a jingle creation, logo design, or business card layout. The buyer would list a job and the payment amount. Gig workers submit their work and the buyer selects the winner.

The third type of gig website is a matching site. Gig workers are matched to buyers determined through a computerized selection process. Each website uses a different set of selection criteria but the goal is to connect buyers with workers who can best meet their needs. Sometimes you can pay a fee to show up more often. Some of these sites offer temporary employment. The company hires you and contracts you out to their customers. This is a temp agency model where you may receive benefits once you reach certain work milestones.

Getting selected for a gig job can be challenging, especially when you are new on a site. How quickly you are chosen depends a lot on the demand for the kind of work you do, how you present yourself to potential buy-ers and your diligence. Check out these great tips below.

Use the App

Download the company's app as soon as you sign up on a gig site. Most apps notify you the instant a new job is posted that requires your skill set. It is extremely important to apply early because in the digital market place speed equals success.

Keep a few files on your cell phone or in the cloud (remote servers that store your files so you can access them from anywhere) so you can use them to bid and apply for gigs. Free cloud storage space can be found at www.dropbox.com, https://mega.nz/, and https://www.pcloud.com/. Have a copy of your resume, a list of your accomplishments, and boilerplate information about who you are at your fingertips. Then you will be able to apply for a job and attach the necessary documentation quickly through your phone.

Capture Attention of Buyers

As mentioned earlier, there is a great deal of competition on some gig websites. Therefore gaining attention can sometimes require diligence, especially when you first start out.

It is important to gather data and use it to make decisions about how you show up on the site. If the site you are working on provides you with information about the top sellers in your line of work, compare their approach to yours. When possible, find out how well your profile is doing. Check out the website community or blog. You can find out how they rank jobseekers. Use that information to make changes.

Keywords and Tags

Many people are confused about tags and keywords. They are very similar. Both are words and phrases people type into a search box or search bar to find information. Tags, however, are labels that identify and organize information.

Tags do not appear in the content while keywords do. Whether a site uses tags or keywords, the bottom line is that they are important for matching you with buyers.

You want to use tags and keywords effectively. For example, if your profile or portfolio is getting low impressions, (i.e., it is not showing up before buyers very often) go back and look at the tags and keywords you are using. Remember, tags and keywords are search terms buyers use to describe what they are looking to purchase. By revisiting your keywords and tags from time to time, you make sure they are delivering what you want.

Examine some of the gigs you qualify for and make sure you are using the same tags and specific keywords that the buyers are using. By doing so, you will receive the right types of alerts when new jobs appear and you will be matched with hiring companies more often.

Powerful Profiles

Your profile is like a digital brochure; it is an introduction to your personal brand. Take your time to make it as appealing as possible. Here are a few suggestions you should consider:

Use a warm inviting photo. You want to be appropriate for your profession and also express your personality. Some sites like www.fiverr.com, www.guru.com and www.golance.com allow you to be very creative with your profile photos. You can use your picture, a screen shot of a website you designed or a picture of your cat if you choose. Be strategic. Your profile is not so much about showcasing what you like as it is about giving the buyers something that appeals to them.

How formal your profile is depends on the type of website you are using. You might want to have a professional photo loaded on websites like www.profinder.com, www.toptal.com and https://talent.hubstaff.com. Creative people be aware. Do not assume that all gig sites in your profession are casual. Take your lead from other people working on the sites.

Feel free to boast in your profile. What have you accomplished? How much money did you save a customer? How did you help position your manager to win big? When possible, create power statements to reflect your measurable, clear achievements. Use formatting to make important information stand out. Here are some examples that might help you create your own statements:

- Weak statement – Implemented new filing system. Power statement – Improved team productivity and operations by overhauling the inefficient filing system, created a logical, clear system and trained staff on its use. Supervisor stated "Our work flow has improved substantially."

- Weak statement – Increased attendance at SENH adult day care center through aggressive marketing. Power statement – Directed a team responsible for an unprecedented 67 percent enrollment increase over 18 months through network marketing, consumer education, and implementation of a highly visible social media campaign that increased our followers on Facebook and Twitter by 110 percent and 30 percent respectively.

If your profile is showing up but buyers are not selecting you, try to figure out why. Make sure you are responding exactly to the buyer's request. Do not assume what they need. Give them what they want.

Look at how you are presenting yourself. Ask yourself: "Am I highlighting myself as an expert? Am I demonstrating how I have successfully solved similar problems? Do I have attachments on my profile along with testimonials showcasing my best work?"

Go back to your competitor's research and compare what they are doing to what you have done. Pose a question to the website community. Ask for honest feedback on your profile and ask for tips on how you can win more jobs. Read the website's frequently asked questions and the new user guide, then experiment with changing things until you create a profile that attracts customers.

Ask the website staff for suggestions. If the telephone number is not listed, use the chat feature or the help service. Ask them to evaluate your profile and recommend how you can make improvements.

Build your portfolio

Another important part of your profile is your portfolio. Your portfolio gives potential buyers a glimpse of the breadth and depth of your work. Choose the items to include very carefully. When possible, make sure the documents you attach prove what you have said. You can include samples of award-winning work, letters of commendations, and a compilation of testimonials from satisfied customers and superiors. Showcase your special training and certifications.

Don't include so many documents that your potential clients get overwhelmed and miss the most pertinent materials. Make sure the documents are current if they have a date on them. Select ones that truly display your brilliance. Remember, you can also link to your work posted on other sites.

Record a one-minute introductory video if you are comfortable and appear well on camera. Highlight your accomplishments and abilities. Or, upload a PowerPoint or slideshow using graphics, photos, testimonials and words to describe your work.

If you use your cell phone to record your video, make sure you have on business attire. You may want to have an office background and make sure there is no audio interference. However, if you don't come across well on camera, do not pursue this option.

Bids That Attract Attention

Most online workers try to submit as many bids as possible. They create a bid response that is general enough to address all of the possible work orders within their line of work. This allows them to apply to requests for bids very quickly. Sound like a good strategy, right? Wrong!

Every bid should be uniquely crafted for the specific request. You can, however, create a template that allows you to customize your bid thus letting the potential client know you have read their request and you can solve their problem quickly and effectively. Let them know you have expertise, complete your assignments on time and that you are a no-drama worker. Here is a template you may consider tweaking.

Hi <name>

I am a <number of years, certifications, etc.> expert in <area in which work is requested.> My rate is typically <dollar amount> but I am flexible.

I am quite interested in <name the buyer's objectives.> In fact, I <name similar work done or problem solved.> My client said <insert short testimonial.> I am sure I can do the same for you quickly and efficiently. If you would like, I can <offer a complementary service and explain the benefits.>

I would like to talk with you further about your needs. Thanks; I look forward to working with you, <your first name>

Let's dissect this template. It includes several features recommended by the top gig workers. It starts by establishing your expertise and your pricing. It's good to let potential buyers know you are willing to negotiate your fees.

Another strategy you can try is providing a price range and saying the cost depends on the details the customer will provide. Be aware, however, some buyers may not prefer this approach because they want a firm bid. So if you try to negotiate after getting further details on the job, don't increase your rate dramatically. That just feels slimy.

This template proves that you read and understand what the potential client is asking and that you have successfully completed similar work. In fact, you even let them know about potential enhancements you can offer to the project.

The quick testimonial adds a nice touch and ensures buyers that you are the person for the job. In closing, you invite them to contact you to discuss the job in more detail.

Great Ratings

Having good ratings is very important. Nothing can top them. They represent your reputation and are an important factor considered by gig sites in matching you with potential customers.

Ask your customers for ratings upfront. And, don't forget to ask for comments also. When possible, ask for a 30-second video testimonial that you can use to promote your work. A short video is worth a thousand words. Here are a couple points that you can ask them to include in the video:

- Their name and company
- Your project
- Your timelines
- Your communication style

- Your work quality
- How well the project was completed

A key for getting positive ratings is excellent customer service and communication. Do a great job and you will receive an excellent rating. When possible, strive to over-deliver for your customers by completing the rush jobs early, or adding a little extra to a job.

I know an editor who formats a cover sheet for jobs that she completes. Although her clients probably create their own layout, just the fact that she made her edit job stand out results in fabulous ratings and customer comments.

Another tip is to bring your offline gigs online. This is especially helpful when you are starting out on a gig website. You can ask existing clients to allow you to run a project through a targeted website. Explain that you really need reviews. You should offer to pay any additional fees that they incur by decreasing your bid. After the job is completed, remind them to write a review.

I have had bidders tell me that they are new to the gig website but they have an outstanding portfolio of work they completed offline. They explained that they were reducing their fees to get established on the site. I was happy to hire them, at a bargain price, and I give them excellent reviews.

Promote your services

Promote your gig work by every means available. I advise my clients to use LinkedIn, Twitter, Instagram and Facebook to talk about their gig work. You don't have to be "salesy" about it. Simple share when you get a new gig, when you finish an interesting gig or when you are looking for new opportunities. If you continue to engage your friends and followers, it won't look like you only reach out to sell yourself.

You also want to consider paying for an ad to display on the social websites where your audience is found. This is a relatively inexpensive way to promote your offering. If you are targeting small businesses for virtual assistance services, you may want to place an ad on LinkedIn. If you are targeting parents for tutoring services, you may want to place an ad and target them on Facebook. Find your audience and direct them back to your online profile.

Finally, consider creating a one-page website and send potential customers there to learn more about you. Free websites are offered by https://www.yola.com, www.weebly.com and www.wix.com. You simply sign up, select a template, start typing in the text boxes and upload files you want to display. This should essentially be a sales page where you highlight your success stories, list the benefits of working with you, upload video testimonials, list awards and certifications and make a personal statement about your dedication to your craft.

Setting Your Rates

Setting rates can be tricky. Experienced workers who are starting online are in an interesting position. You may be competing against people who are less experienced and charge lesser rates.

In the consulting world rates are equivalent to the impact of the problem you solve, your years of experience and the time it takes to produce the solution. For example, I hired a photographer who produces picture perfect photos. I pay her a higher rate because of her expertise even though she is slower than another photographer that I had tried.

If you know how to communicate your value, then your ideal client will pay more. But you may consider lowering your fees until you get established online. In any event, you need to know the going rate first. Here are some tactics for determining the going rate for what you offer:

- Google it. Do a search on pricing guides for your profession. It's surprising what you can learn.
- Go to resources like www.glassdoor.com and your industry trade organizations.
- Search gig websites. Often you can find blog posts and articles about pricing. You can also ask in your community or help sections of the website.
- Ask your client what they budgeted for a particular job. This may not be what the job is really worth on the open market but it gives you a starting point.
- Ask friends in your industry. They probably will share their rates or at least let you know if they think you are too high or too low.
- Read trade publications and articles. You can frequently learn more about prices there. You could also join industry networking groups where these issues are discussed.

This chapter presented winning tips you can use to secure gigs. You have learned about tag words, creating your profile and selecting items for your portfolio. Implementing those that work for you and you will soon be hustling online.

CHAPTER 10

Big Change is in the Air: The Rapid Transition of The Gig Economy

Digital gig work is changing everything, everywhere. Regulations are becoming antiquated as you read this book. Currently, rules in one nation do not necessarily apply when workers find gig work across country borders. Government regulators are baffled and uncertain about how to craft guidance that won't need to be modified before the ink dries.

Every month opportunities to find gig work grows and changes. The implications of this changing economy are massive. The way we think about "work" is morphing quickly. This level of global opportunity and competition has never been seen before.

This chapter alerts you to some of the current discussions. As mentioned earlier, the state of affairs is changing rapidly. Before this book is printed, there is a real possibility that some new development or insight will be released.

As a gig worker, whether full-time or part-time, you want to be aware of the laws, regulations and trends that impact the way you work, your benefits and your pay.

Keep your eyes open because change is in the air. This chapter, overviews the landscape when this book was written. You are encouraged to stay abreast of these issues and new ones as they emerge.

Employment Status

Misclassification of workers is a big deal, especially to the IRS. In the not too distant past, it was much clearer. Employees worked at the office, for a specified number of hours, using the employers' tools and received a regular paycheck.

Contractors were hired to do a job and worked when they wanted, where they wanted and how they wanted as long as the work was satisfactory. They were paid when certain milestones were met as specified by a contract.

Today all of this is quite muddy. As a result, gig companies like Lyft, Grubhub and Uber have been sued several times as the workers insist upon employee status. If you want to expand your business beyond online gig work, make it easy for companies to hire you as a contractor.

Be sure to operate as a business – set up a website, use a company name, file for the EIN (employer identification number) from the Internal Revenue Service, print business cards, etc.[1] By doing so you minimize the perception of being viewed as an employee and buyers feel like they have added protection from IRS misclassification audits.

Wages and Benefits

Gig workers are independent contractors and therefore have no pay foundation. In other words, they are paid according to their negotiation skills. Minimum wage laws do not apply to contractors. Recently, nonetheless, there is an outcry that workers are deliberately being under-paid by being misclassified as contractors.

For example, suppose a gig worker is considered a contractor and accepts a job that takes ten hours to complete but she contracted for only $50 of pay. Some argue this is a problem that is creating economic instability for the contract worker. In the past, accepting low bids or under-estimating how long a job would take was simply considered a poor business practice.

Similarly, benefits are only available to employees. Consequently, many full-time gig workers do without benefits such as health insurance, sick leave and retire-ment, vacation and others because they can't afford them. Several states and organizations are looking at various ways to finance benefits for gig workers.

New York is looking at a tax on the gig transaction to create portable benefits similar to what it did for limo drivers in the late 1990s. Others states like Washington State and New Jersey are looking at a program whereby the buyers would contribute to funds for contractors.

This effort to support gig workers may backfire, how-ever. In some cases these laws may make the American gig worker too expensive and companies may opt to ac-quire talent from overseas where there are no such re-quirements. These types of regulation might result in the American gig worker having more options for benefits but less income to pay for them. Stay tuned.

Today, nonetheless, gig workers must purchase their own benefits. Health insurance, disability policies and re-tirement accounts are available but are quite expensive because there are no group discounts offered for individual plans.

There are organizations like the Freelancers Union that offer a benefits platform for gig workers (https://www.freelancersunion.org/benefits). Benefits are also available through professional organizations, the federal Health Insurance Marketplace created by the Affordable Care Act or Obamacare (https://www.healthcare.gov/self-employed/coverage). This insurance is currently being debated and possibly replaced.

Lack of Representation

Unlike employees, gig workers cannot form organized groups or unions to bargain with the employer on their behalf. Currently, gig companies can penalize the worker for violating their policies without any discussion. In fact, many workers on gig websites report having their accounts frozen or deleted without an opportunity to defend themselves. This is why it's important to understand the website you choose to work on.

Taxes

Many gig workers are not paying quarterly taxes as required. For some, it is because they don't understand their tax obligations and others simply do not set aside the resources to pay their taxes. Basically, if you intend to make a profit with your gig activities, then you may owe taxes.[2] You need to connect with a tax expert for specifics.

In addition, the laws are changing around income gained online. In fact, internet sales income tax is one issue you need to watch very closely because it is being debated right now. In the past, internet income was exempt from state taxes unless you had a physical operation in the state.[3] This might be changing. Speak with a tax expert.

References

[1] Rafter, M. (2018). *Who are you, gig worker or employee?* Sandiegouniontribune.com. Accessed 6 Feb. 2018: http://www.sandiegouniontribune.com/business/technology/sd-fi-labor-blurred-lines-20170807-story.html.

[2] Irs.gov. (2018). *Self Employed Individuals Tax Center | Internal Revenue Service.* Accessed 6 Feb. 2018: https://www.irs.gov/businesses/small-businesses-self-employed/self-employed-individuals-tax-center.

[3] Smallbusiness.chron.com. (2018). *Do I Have to Pay Taxes for an Internet Business?* Accessed 6 Feb. 2018: http://smallbusiness.chron.com/pay-taxes-internet-business-4058.html.

Part III: Proceed

To carry on or continue any action or process, to go on to do something, to continue one's discourse. (dictionary.com)

CHAPTER 11

Seven Final Recommendations

As a mature worker, you are now prepared to deal with one aspect of the gig economy – online gig websites. You understand why you need to think differently about work and the importance of renewing your mind accordingly. You also know that the gig economy is here to stay, thanks to technology.

You completed a step-by-step process to assess your talents (what you were born with), skills (what you have learned along the way) and your passions (that dream that just won't die) and find the sweet spot where they all intersect in the marketplace. Then, you walked through the steps for selecting gig sites to start exploring.

Once you enter the gig economy, you enter the door to entrepreneurism. Some of you may not be familiar with what all this means. That is why you reviewed the business side of gig work and the tools you need to succeed. Finally, I provide a massive resource of gig websites for you to choose from in the next chapter, The Digital Marketplace.

This final chapter of content summarizes seven final recommendations that will help you thrive as a gig worker. Some of the information provided, you may have already heard before. Don't gloss over it. Sometimes the difference between success and failure is listening to the commonly-understood wisdom and practices of pioneers who have gone before you.

Lastly, this book ends with a number of bonus materials. Use the resources provided as you embark upon this new journey. Join the Facebook group, Baby Boomers Make Money, (www.facebook.com/groups/BabyBoomersMakeMoney/) to learn and connect with others who are charting their own course. Check out the additional free resources available at www.AngelaHeathSpeaks.com. If I can help you in any way, just holler.

This is an exciting time for you. In mid-life, you have the opportunity to do what you love, when you want to do it and without anyone looking over your shoulders. So, whether your gig work is part-time, fulltime or intermittent, I wish you the best of luck. Use these finals suggestions to seal the deal!

Recommendation One – The Time is Now

You must start now because time will not wait. If not, you could soon look up and one year, five years, or ten years will have passed and all you will have is regret. It's important to start today; in fact, you may want to start right now. I hate to be the bearer of bad news but people 45-plus and older probably have fewer years ahead to finally live their life purpose than they have behind them.

Many times people hesitate because they believe they need to have everything right before they start. No you don't! You will never have everything you need. Start with what you have – decades of experience, contacts in your industry, skills, talents, hobbies, intuition, references etc. – and figure out the rest along the way.

90

The platforms listed have already done 80 percent of the heavy lifting. You simply have to register and get started offering your talents, skills and abilities to an international marketplace.

Recommendation Two – Manage Your Spending

There are a couple things you can do to minimize your output before you begin to scale or grow a business. Avoid spending a lot of money as you get started. Buy only what's needed; you don't have to buy everything. Purchase for the business phase you are in. When you grow, you purchase more. A few ideas for managing your spending include:

- Buy things secondhand or inexpensively. Auction sites are a great way to find equipment, office sup-plies and merchandize to sell at a discount.
- Barter with people. You give them something; they give you something. It's a win-win.
- Borrow things you need until you're ready to actu-ally purchase it on your own.
- Use free stock photo sites such as www.pixabay. com or www.pexels.com for free photographs.
- Do a Google search for whatever you need using the word "free" before the item that you want. Often-times, you will find a free or inexpensive resource.

Recommendation Three - Don't Go It Alone

Get the help that you need. It makes no sense for you to try to do everything. When you try to do everything, you do nothing well. Usually you end up wasting a lot of valuable time to poorly produce something outside of your area of expertise.

When people are looking for high-priced things, appearances matter. You want to make sure you don't go it alone. Get the help that you need.

To secure expert assistance, often you can barter. Simply offer your skills and talents to others in exchange for their help. You do something for them, they do something for you. Sometimes, it's just a matter of asking.

You can also get high quality by using low-cost services. Go to some of the freelance websites that are suggested in this book, you'll be able to find people who will do all kinds of things for you and they're not going to charge you an arm and a leg.

Remember, my company can help guide you. This book is just one of the many resources that we make available to experienced workers who want to pursue opportunities to make money by using what they already know. See the bonus section for discounts on our training and mentoring services.

Recommendation Four – Create a Plan

Let's be clear. Just because I recommend starting now doesn't mean jump in without a plan. Create a logical and achievable plan; given the time and energy you have available.

Don't let the plan evolve into an excuse to avoid action, however. Your plan does not have to be long and detailed. Start by planning for the next four to six months and have one or two main objectives. Each week, identify one thing to learn and one thing to complete.

Recommendation Five - Work on One Platform

Sure, you may be ambitious and want to build an online empire right away. However, you will want to start working on one platform at a time. Master making money on one website and then expand to others.

Learn the platform. Go through the website tutorials. Be attentive. You may want to listen, watch, read and then practice the skill that was taught. You may want to create your own cheat sheets and use an up-to-date reference book. This approach helps you to rapidly gain understanding of how the website functions and shortcuts that lead to making money quicker.

Recommendation Six – Become Known as an Expert

Depending on what you are going to offer, it may be helpful to establish your credibility. For example, if you're selling a skill or talent, being known as an expert on the topic will cause people to want to hire you.

Thought leadership allows you to charge more and sell more. People pay more for experts than they do for amateurs. Here are four helpful suggestions for establishing your thought leadership taken from our course, *Legends are Made*. I also recommend that you read the book, *You Everywhere Now* by Mike Koenig. It's an excellent read.

- Join groups where the influencers in your industry congregate including local Meet Ups, local social groups and charities, trade association meetings, etc.

- Join the online discussion about cutting edge approaches and trends in your industry. Don't simply read blogs and listen to podcasts, make comments, offer solutions and a different point of view. Become a valuable member of the community.
- Become the leader. Start a Facebook community, YouTube channel or start your own blog. You could even ask a thought leader to contribute from time to time. Invite people to join and post on a regular basis.
- Use www.klout.com to measure your social influence. It's exciting to watch your influence increase.

Recommendation Seven - Study Success

Once you experience success, document exactly what you did from the beginning to the end. Analyze your results. Examine the keywords, photos and graphics used, your description of the offering and who purchased from you. Try to figure out the success factors and then repeat those.

You can also replicate some of the elements your top competitors use. Often, large companies research which colors, font, key words, etc. are the most successful. They spend tens of thousands of dollars testing to improve sales. You can replicate some of their tactics, without violating any ethical or legal regulations.

Conclusion

In conclusion, I just want to encourage you, don't be afraid. There is no way you can live to be 45-plus without having something of value to offer in the marketplace. You can do this.

This book takes some of the mystery out of making money by using what you already know. Now, you know it does not have to be expensive at all. By using existing websites, you can begin making money in a matter of hours.

So, why not take action today? You really don't have a lot of time to waste. You don't have to fumble around like I did for six or seven years. This resource offers shortcuts to start making money quickly.

People are looking for what you have to offer right now. They are willing to pay if you are willing to sell. Why not give people what they want?

Please share your success with us at info@ tkcincorporated.com. We are happy to support you in any way possible.

Happy Hustle!

CHAPTER 12

The Digital Marketplace:
Endless Possibilities

Welcome to the digital gig website marketplace! Selling your time and talents online can be very profitable and offer freedom and flexibility. But where do you start? This chapter is a compilation of websites where you can find buyers who are looking for your talents, skills, and passions.

Certainly, this is not a complete list because, as explained earlier, these websites come and go. The possibilities are endless as new sites appear weekly. This list is updated every six months. You can make a onetime update request by registering your book purchase at www.AngelaHeathSpeaks.com. If you want to add a great gig website to the list, send an email to info@ tkcincorporated.com.

PLEASE NOTE – We do not endorse any of the sites listed. In addition, we do not warrant the information shared about the websites. The information found in these chapters comes from the company's website pages or was provided by a website representative who responded to our industry survey. In deciding which gig websites to include, we considered the following criteria:

referrals by credible sources, media coverage, existence of an active community, availability of names of company contacts available and social media presence.

To help you quickly find gig sites that you can use, they are categorized into ten sections based on how they describe themselves. As you expand your gig operations, you may revisit this list to identify other categories and sites that are a good fit for your skill set. Again, we recommend that you learn about a site before you share your profile. Remember to practice good consumer techniques that we described earlier.

SECTION 1
ADMIN

In the admin category you will find opportunities to do work related to call centers, customer service, data entry, transcription, virtual assistant and web research. Many of these listings are for remote workers meaning you would work from the comfort of your home. Many of the websites listed are job boards and others will match you with opportunities. You may need to get a background check for certain positions and be tested for others.

In addition to these gig sites, many companies are constantly looking for part-time employees and contractors to complete administrative work. If you are interested in a particular company, check to see if they have any contracting or virtual gigs.

24/7 Virtual Assistant
www.247virtualassistants.com
Get matched with a virtual assistant position that caters to your skill set.
FOCUS: Administrative work, customer service, web development, data entry, marketing

Allied Universal
www.aus.com
Work with recruiters to get matched with a temporary job that is right for your skill set.
FOCUS: Administrative, professional, light industrial

Arise Virtual Solutions
www.arise.com
Start your own call center, select a client from the list, learn their system, and start the project.
FOCUS: Call center, customer service

ASC Services

www.fdch.com
Contract opportunities in various industries in the Washington D.C. area.
FOCUS: Political transcription, proofreading, translation

BSG Clearing

www.bsgclearing.com/contact_us/careers/live-operator-independent-contractor
Work from home as a live operator as needed.
FOCUS: Live operator

ContractWorld

www.contractxchange.com
Work as a virtual customer service agent from the comfort of your own home.
FOCUS: Customer service

CoWorks

www.coworks.com
Coworks recruiters match you with freelance opportunities within the Cowork platform.
FOCUS: Administrative

Expedict

www.expedict.com/19-employment-enquiry
Jobs are available for experienced audio typists on an as-needed basis.
FOCUS: Audio typists

Fancy Hands

www.fancyhands.com
Complete personal assistant tasks for people all over the United States from your home.
FOCUS: Personal assistant

Gengo

www.gengo.com/translators
Translation work available.
FOCUS: Translation

LiveOps

www.join.liveops.com/work-from-home-call-center-jobs
Set your own hours and pick your projects as a virtual customer service agent.
FOCUS: Customer service

Money Making Mommy

www.moneymakingmommy.com
A website dedicated to sharing legitimate work from home positions.
FOCUS: Customer service, marketing, editing/writing, translation, data entry

Net Transcripts

www.nettranscripts.com/careers.htm
Search for contractor transcription job opportunities.
FOCUS: Transcription

Online Jobs

www.onlinejobs.ph
Become a virtual assistant and work remotely.
FOCUS: Administrative, development, customer service, design, marketing

Production Transcripts

www.productiontranscripts.com/employment-opportunities-in-transcription
Apply to be a transciptionist with Production Transcripts.
FOCUS: Transciption

Rat Race Rebellion

www.ratracerebellion.com
A list of available work from home administrative jobs.
FOCUS: Telemarketing, customer service, transcription

SpeakWrite

cms.speakwrite.com/WEB/sw/employment/typist/typist-home.aspx?popup=y
Apply to be a transcriptionist.
FOCUS: Transcription

Sykes

www.sykes.com/whitepapers/home-based-agents
Work from home as a customer service agent.
FOCUS: Customer service

Ten til Two

www.tentiltwo.com
A job board for part time office jobs in Colorado.
FOCUS: Part time office work

Vicky Virtual Receptionists

www.vickyvirtual.com/join-team
Work from home answering phone calls for various businesses.
FOCUS: Administrative

Virtual Office Temps

www.virtualassistantjobs.com
Become a virtual assistant, showcase your skills, and bid on available jobs.
FOCUS: Administrative, design, communications, accounting

Vitac

www.vitac.com/careers
Find and apply for remote captioning positions.
FOCUS: Captioning for medical accessibility

Working Solutions

https://jobs.workingsolutions.com
Apply to be a customer service agent and work from home.
FOCUS: Customer service

Worldwide101

www.worldwide101.com/jobs
Apply to be a virtual assistant and get matched with projects.
FOCUS: Administrative, marketing, customer service, project management

Zirtual

www.zirtual.com
Find virtual assistant jobs in the United States.
FOCUS: Virtual assistant

SECTION 2
BUSINESS

Business websites are also very popular. Many companies look for interim expert talent and special business skills for a specific project or objective. Jobs are available for all types of business skills including advertising, accounting, business consulting, customer relationship management, e-commerce, email marketing, financial management, human resources, lead generation, market research, PR, sales, and social media management.

Huge areas of growth include digital marketing and social media management. Positions are inside corporations as well as remote. As more large corporations turn to the gig economy to fill temporary positions, these jobs will definitely increase. Job boards as well as bid and match gig sites are available.

Angel List
www.angel.co
Find a job at a startup, see salary upfront, apply privately.
FOCUS: Development, marketing, sales, product management

Business Talent Group
www.businesstalentgroup.com
Provide your technical expertise to companies and projects in your field.
FOCUS: Automotive, healthcare, media, non-profit, financial, hospitality

Catalant
www.gocatalant.com
Bid on various freelance positions and work with global clients, including the Fortune 100.
FOCUS: Human resources, marketing, business, operations

Cerius Executives

www.ceriusexecutives.com

Job seekers with executive-level experience can choose from an array of opportunities.

FOCUS: Sales, finance, human resources, marketing, executive management

Experfy

www.experfy.com

Become a solutions provider and work on big data projects with clients all over the globe.

FOCUS: Big data consultants

Expert 360

www.expert360.com

Find and bid on consulting jobs in a variety of industries, projects, and contract lengths.

FOCUS: Marketing, human resources, sales, accounting

Gerson Lehrman Group

www.glg.it

Become a Council Member and share your expertise on various subjects with companies.

FOCUS: Consulting

Gigwalk

www.gigwalk.com

Find local business field research gigs.

FOCUS: Business research assistance

M Squared Consulting

www.msquared.com

Find permanent and interim consulting positions.

FOCUS: Business consulting

Naming Force

www.namingforce.com

Compete in contests to help clients name their projects, companies or products.

FOCUS: Marketing

Patina Solutions

www.patinasolutions.com
A firm that offers project-based and interim employment to professionals with 25 or more years of experience.
FOCUS: Consulting, advisory, management

SkillBridge

www.toptal.com/finance
Apply to be a finance expert and share your knowledge to help companies grow and become successful.
FOCUS: Finance, interim CFO, startup funding support

SpareHire

www.sparehire.com
Create a profile and bid on jobs/projects that match your background and skillset.
FOCUS: Banking, management consulting, finance, corporate development

Tatum

www.tatum-us.com
Help companies solve challenges, create change, and drive growth.
FOCUS: Project management, consulting

YourEncore

www.yourencore.com
Retirees and/or experienced professionals can find rewarding consulting project work.
FOCUS: Consulting

Zintro

www.zintro.com/home
Get matched with relevant opportunties and help businesses solve a specific challenge.
FOCUS: Consulting

SECTION 3
CREATIVE

If you work in the creative arena, there are numerous gigs available on several gig platforms. These jobs include animation, audio production, graphic design, illustration, logo creation, package design, photography, PowerPoint, video production and voice over work. Many of the sites run creative contests where you bid on a job by presenting your work. Buyers then decide which concepts they want. You will also find job boards and sites that match you with buyers.

99Designs
www.99designs.com
A freelance community where you can compete in contests to win jobs.
FOCUS: Graphic design

Aquent
www.aquent.com
Directly apply for creative positions worldwide, or connect through the staffing agency to get matched with a client.
FOCUS: Creative, marketing, technical

Awesome web
www.awesomeweb.com
A freelance community, where you pay a monthly fee to have projects come to you instead of bidding.
FOCUS: Design, development

Behance
www.behance.net/joblist
A job board for creative and development professionals.
FOCUS: Graphic design, web design, web development, writing

Clever
www.realclever.com
Find and apply for creative jobs with a marketing agency.
FOCUS: Photography, video, blogging, writing

Create My Tattoo
www.createmytattoo.com
Submit your tattoo designs in contests that fit your skillset.
FOCUS: Tattoo artistry

Dribble
www.dribbble.com/jobs
A job board just for designers.
FOCUS: Graphic design

Fiverr
www.fiverr.com
Join Fiverr, create a gig, and accept proposals from clients who
need your services.
FOCUS: Graphic design, writing, marketing, web development

Get Photography Jobs
www.getphotographyjobs.com/job-seekers/job-search.php
Find short term and permanent photography positions throughout
the United States
FOCUS: Photography

Gigster
www.gigster.com
Apply to be designers and/or developers and get contract work
for projects that meet your skillset.
FOCUS: Design, development

I Love Creatives
www.ilovecreatives.com
Find jobs, events, or spaces to showcase your creative skills.
FOCUS: Design, development, marketing, culinary

Jobscribe
www.jobscribe.com

Sign up for their newsletter to receive listings of remote positions at tech startups.
FOCUS: Design, development, marketing, mobile apps

Loom
www.loom.co
Work on projects and choose to get paid in cash, equity, or both.
FOCUS: Design, development, branding

Matador
www.marketplace.matadoru.com/journalists
Find writing, photography, and video freelance opportunities.
FOCUS: Writing, photography, video

Media Bistro
www.mediabistro.com/jobs
A job board for positions in the media industry.
FOCUS: Design, production, marketing, development, writing

Modsquad
www.modsquad.com
Get matched with projects and work as much or as little as you want.
FOCUS: Digital engagement, social media work

Moonlighting
www.moonlighting.com
Find part-time or freelance positions near you.
FOCUS: Design, marketing, video, editing/writing, development

Patreon
www.patreon.com/
Get paid for creating things. Create a page, get fans, get paid.
FOCUS: Music, videos, podcasts

PickyDomains
www.pickydomains.com
Compete in contests to help clients create domain names and slogans. Win the contest and get paid.
FOCUS: Creative

Skyword

https://create.skyword.com/contributorJoin.action
Get connected with companies looking for top-notch creative services.
FOCUS: Writing, development, design, video

SmartShoot

www.smartshoot.com
Find and apply for photography and video jobs.
FOCUS: Photography, video, filmmaking, customer service, development

The Creative Loft

https://photography.thecreativeloft.com/
Join this community and gain access to photography jobs all over the country.
FOCUS: Photography

Working Not Working

www.workingnotworking.com
Find and bid on creative projects with big-name companies.
FOCUS: Design, creative, photography, production

SECTION 4
GENERAL AND 50-PLUS GIG SITES

Every reader will want to visit the general and 50-plus gig sites. This is by far the largest category of websites with the broadest selection of jobs. General and 50-plus gig sites list all types of opportunities.

There are quite a few job boards in the category as well as opportunities to bid on jobs. Some of these general sites are huge and competitive. Consequently, they may offer special promotional options for an additional fee. It gives you an advantage by presenting your profile to buyers more often.

The 50-plus gig websites, however, are targeted to mature workers. The buyers are looking for experienced people to complete the work without a steep learning curve. These buyers are making a commitment to hiring older gig workers by listing their jobs on these specific websites.

American Airlines
https://jobs.aa.com
View and apply for positions at American Airlines.
FOCUS: Customer service, pilots, professional, IT

Career Builder
www.careerbuilder.com
Job board for part-time and full-time positions across a variety of industries.
FOCUS: Hospitality, technology, business, education, professional

CoolWorks.com
www.coolworks.com
A job board that lists "cool" jobs in national parks, at beaches and adventure sites.

FOCUS: Administrative, hospitality, education, retail, volunteer/ non-profit

Flex Jobs
www.flexjobs.com
Find flexible, part-time and/or telecommunting jobs.
FOCUS: Administrative, education, business, graphic design, customer service

Flex Professionals
www.flexprofessionalsllc.com
Part-time, full-time and virtual positions available in Boston and Washington DC.
FOCUS: Administrative, accounting, legal

Freelanced
www.freelanced.com
A freelance social network where you can find and bid on available projects.
FOCUS: Graphic design, administrative, writing, marketing, consulting

Freelancer
www.Freelancer.com
Bid on projects that match your skill set.
FOCUS: Design, development, writing, marketing, administrative

Freelancermap
www.freelancermap.com
Apply for contract or short term positions through their job board.
FOCUS: Development, graphic design, engineering, IT

Glassdoor
www.glassdoor.com
View and apply for positions in a variety of industries throughout the United States.
FOCUS: Administrative, accounting, legal, marketing, design

Go Lance
www.golance.com
Create a profile, bid on projects, and earn money at home to fit your schedule.

FOCUS: Accounting, consulting, customer service, design, engineering and IT

Greatlance
www.greatlance.com
Create a profile, bid on projects, and earn money at home on your own schedule.
FOCUS: Administrative, translation, customer service, photography

Guru
www.guru.com
Find and bid on various industry projects. Earn as little or as much right from your own home.
FOCUS: Administrative, design, management, finance, marketing

Hire My Mom
www.hiremymom.com
Work from home jobs for moms. Projects range in industry, skillset, and length.
FOCUS: Administrative, marketing, customer service

Hubstaff Talent
http://talent.hubstaff.com
Create a profile and let employers find you and your skillset.
FOCUS: Design, development, marketing, administrative

IEEE Job Site
jobs.ieee.org
IEEE members can browse and apply for jobs related to engineering, science and IT.
FOCUS: Science, networking, computer engineering

iFreelance
www.ifreelance.com
Create a profile, bid on projects, and keep 100% of your earnings.
FOCUS: Administrative, accounting, design, marketing, photography

Indeed
www.indeed.com
A job board for professionals of all backgrounds.
FOCUS: Accounting, administrative, marketing, development, design

JobBoardNetwork

www.jobboardnetwork.com

A job board where you can find a variety of jobs.

FOCUS: Accounting, agriculture, childcare, retail, customer service

Jobs UPS

www.jobs-ups.com

View and apply for posiitions at UPS.

FOCUS: Drivers, retail

Jobspresso

www.jobspresso.co

A job board for remote positions.

FOCUS: Tech, marketing, customer support

Kelly Services

www.kellyservices.us

Find jobs in various sectors throughout the United States.

FOCUS: Administrative, healthcare, human resources, retail, engineering

Konsus

www.konsus.com/career

Remote positions available.

FOCUS: Design, project management, data entry

LinkedIn Profinder

www.linkedin.com/profinder/pros

Get matched with positions that fit your expertise and bid on the projects.

FOCUS: Wide variety of professional opportunities

LiveCareer

www.livecareer.com

Create an account to get help building your resume and find jobs that fit your skillset.

FOCUS: Administrative, hospitality, marketing, human resources, medical

Local Solo
www.LocalSolo.com
Apply for projects, contracts and full time jobs.
FOCUS: Design, development, marketing, copywriting, mobile apps

McKinsey & Company Careers
www.mckinsey.com/careers/search-jobs
View and apply for part time positions and project work.
FOCUS: Administrative, marketing, communications, legal, human resouces

MeFi Jobs
https.//jobs.metafilter.com
Thousands of freelance jobs throughout the world.
FOCUS: Administrative, human resources, hospitality, writing

Monster
www.monster.com
A job board with positions in a variety of fields, locations and experience levels.
FOCUS: Administrative, human resources, hospitality, writing, marketing

Next Job at Home
www.nextjobathome.com
Find and apply for work-from-home/remote job opportunities in a variety of industries.
FOCUS: Data entry, customer service, writing, design, development

One Space Freelancers
www.onespace.com
Work on as many or as little freelance projects as you want.
FOCUS: Writing, editing, data entry, product research

Outsourcely
www.outsourcely.com
Apply for long-term remote positions in a variety of fields.
FOCUS: Marketing, design, development, administrative

Over 50 Job Board

www.over50jobboard.com

A job board for job seekers over 50.

FOCUS: Administrative, retail, marketing, accounting, medical

People Per Hour

www.peopleperhour.com

Submit proposals for projects and get paid when you finish the job.

FOCUS: Photography, copywriting, translation, design, development

Power to Fly

www.powertofly.com/jobs

Look for positions at companies that empower women.

FOCUS: Design, development, marketing, administrative, accounting

Prime CB

http://prime.cbtechnology.com

A job board for seniors and baby boomers.

FOCUS: Healthcare, customer service, sales, marketing, IT

Remote.Co

www.remote.co/remote-jobs

Find remote jobs in a variety of industries and skill sets.

FOCUS: Sales, customer service, accounting, project management, writing

Remotive

www.remotive.io/find-a-job

A job board for remote jobs anywhere in the world.

FOCUS: Marketing, development, sales, support, human resources

Retired Brains

www.retiredbrains.com/index.html

A job board for job seekers in retirement.

FOCUS: Retail, editing, transcription, direct selling

Retiree Work Force

www.retireeworkforce.com

A job board for job seekers in retirement.

FOCUS: Customer service, drivers, accounting, hospitality

Retirement Jobs

www.retirementjobs.com
A job board for job seekers in retirement.
FOCUS: Marketing, hospitality, driver, healthcare

Senior Job Bank

www.seniorjobbank.org
A job board for job seekers over the age of 50.
FOCUS: Customer service, retail, hospitality

Senior Service America

www.seniorserviceamerica.org
Employment programs for disadvantaged and low-income job seekers over 50 in the United States.
FOCUS: Agriculture, administrative, science, QA

Seniors 4 hire

www.seniors4hire.org
Job seekers over 50 can find and apply for positions throughout the world.
FOCUS: Customer service, IT, sales, design, finance

Simply Hired

www.simplyhired.com
Discover local jobs, estimate salaries and apply for jobs that match your skillset.
FOCUS: Accounting, administrative, marketing, sales, human resources, healthcare

Sitel

https://www.sitel.com/careers
View and apply for positions in a variety of areas.
FOCUS: Customer services, IT, marketing, sales,

Skip The Drive

www.skipthedrive.com
A job board for remote and telecommuting jobs.
FOCUS: Accounting, customer service, development, healthcare, sales

Snag a Job
www.snagajob.com
Find hourly jobs at companies throughout the United States. Find part-time, seasonal, full-time, various shifts and more.
FOCUS: Customer service, retail, hospitality, education, healthcare

Speedlancer
https://speedlancer.recruiterbox.com
Find remote and in-person freelance positions.
FOCUS: Writing, video, design, data entry

Style Careers
http://stylecareers.com/
Find opportunities in the fashion world by connecting with professionals in the industry.
FOCUS: Fashion designer, photography, branding, advertising

Temporary & Part time Jobs
www.tempandparttimejobs.com
A job board for retirees.
FOCUS: A wide variety of jobs in many industries.

The Balance
www.thebalance.com
Find and apply for positions at the balance.
FOCUS: Writing, design, development

The Flexwork for Women Alliance
9livesforwomen.com/the-flexwork-women-alliance/
A list of firms that help women find flexible jobs.
FOCUS: Marketing, sales, legal, administrative

The Muse
www.themuse.com/jobs
A job board with a variety of positions in various cities. Can also read company reviews and get career advice.
FOCUS: Administrative, development, sales, design, banking

Total Jobs
www.totaljobs.com
Apply for a variety of jobs across industries and functions on this job board.
FOCUS: Accounting, marketing, design, retail, customer service

United State Courts
www.uscourts.gov/careers/search-judiciary-jobs
Find jobs within the federal courts and federal public defender organizations.
FOCUS: Legal, administrative, accounting, human resources, IT

Upwork
www.upwork.com
Create a profile listing your skills and bid on jobs.
FOCUS: Design, development, administrative, data entry, marketing

US Contract Staff
www.uscontractstaff.com
Get matched with temporary or direct-to-hire opportunities.
FOCUS: Administrative, data entry, sales

USA Jobs
www.usajobs.gov
Find various positions available with the U.S.government.
FOCUS: Engineering, computer science, human resources, mathematics, healthcare

Virtual Vocations
www.virtualvocations.com
Find telecommuting jobs in a variety of sectors.
FOCUS: Accounting, administrative, healthcare, design, marketing, IT

We Work Remotely
www.weworkremotely.com
Find and apply for remote/work-from-home positions.
FOCUS: Programming, customer service, marketing, engineering

Wit Mart
www.witmart.com
Find and bid on projects that match your skillset.

FOCUS: Design, writing, marketing, development

Women for Hire
www.womenforhire.com
A website geared towards helping women find positions that fit their skills.
FOCUS: Marketing, retail, administrative, sales, legal

Work at Home Women
www.theworkathomewoman.com
This site lists a wide variety of jobs nationwide.
FOCUS: Work at home

Work Force 50
https://jobs.workforce50.com
A job board for retirees and older workers looking for positions.
FOCUS: Transporation, retail, administrative, customer service, human resources

Working Nomads
www.workingnomads.co/jobs
Find remote positions that allow you to work from home or anywhere in the world.
FOCUS: Development, management, writing, education, human resources

WorkMarket
www.workmarket.com
A matching service for part-time and seasonal support that offers additional resources.
FOCUS: Computer systems, transcribing, proof reading

ZipRecruiter
www.ziprecruiter.com
A job board for local, remote, part-time, and full-time positions in various industries.
FOCUS: Administrative, customer service, healthcare, marketing, retail

SECTION 5
INTERNATIONAL

For people interested in working on temporary assignments in different parts of the world, the international section will be helpful. The type of jobs offered vary and include everything from business, to teaching English to technology to labor positions. Some jobs are remote but many require you to live in the country during your employment. Most of these websites are job boards.

Adzuna
https://www.adzuna.co.za
A job board with an array of positions in South Africa.
FOCUS: Accounting, consulting, customer service, IT, retail

BackDoorJobs.com
www.backdoorjobs.com
A variety of opportunities to work abroad.
FOCUS: Teaching, volunteering, hospitality, environmental

Canadian Freelance Writing Jobs
www.freelancewritingjobs.ca
Listing of freelance writing opportunities in Canada.
FOCUS: Article writing and blogging

Fish Talent
www.fishtalent.com
Create a shop and sell your creative services in India.
FOCUS: Design, writing, marketing, translation, development

Gumtree
www.gumtree.com/jobs
View and apply for various industry positions in the UK.
FOCUS: Administrative, accounting, healthcare, construction, customer service

Go Overseas

www.gooverseas.com/teaching-jobs-abroad
Go abroad and teach students of all ages. Teaching gigs can be short-term or long-term.
FOCUS: Teaching

Hostel Travel Jobs

www.hosteltraveljobs.com
Work in top travel destinations at hotels and hostels.
FOCUS: Hospitality

Jobsdb.com

www.jobsdb.com
Search jobs in Hong Kong, Indonesia, Singapore and Thailand.
FOCUS: Accounting, human resources, legal, marketing, medical

JobStreets

www.jobstreet.com.ph
A job board for professionals looking for positions in the Philippines.
FOCUS: Accounting, sales, hospitality, IT, science

Modern Day Nomads

www.moderndaynomads.com
A job board for those who desire to travel while still using their creative talents.
FOCUS: Culinary, media, design, hospitality

Monster UK

www.monster.co.uk
A job board with positions in the UK offering a variety of functions, industries and levels of experience.
FOCUS: Administrative, human resources, hospitality, writing, marketing

Reed

www.reed.co.uk
Find temporary and permanent positions in the UK on this job board.
FOCUS: Accounting, administrative, engineering, healthcare, marketing

SEEK

www.seek.com.au

A job board in Austrailia for positions in various industries, skillsets, and job types.

FOCUS: Accounting, healthcare, sales, marketing, consulting

Simply Law Jobs

www.simplylawjobs.com/jobs

Find legal positions in the UK and Asia.

FOCUS: Legal

Transcom

https://applications.transcom.com/OnlineEmploymentApplication/main.aspx

Find and apply for customer service positions.

FOCUS: International customer service

WFH.IO

www.wfh.io

A job board for remote digital and tech jobs in Canada.

FOCUS: Design, marketing, development, engineering

Work Abroad

www.workabroad.ph

A job board that helps Filipino job seekers find job overseas.

FOCUS: Customer service, healthcare, administrative, marketing

SECTION 6
OTHER

Websites listed under the Other section provide unique opportunities. Here you will find jobs in fulfillment centers, cooking, focus group participation, product testing, agriculture, home improvement and more. You may find an unusual opportunity that might be of interest.

2020 Research
https://join.2020panel.com/page/1
Make money online or in-person by giving your opinion in surveys, focus groups, or interviews.
FOCUS: Surveys, focus groups, online discussions

Amazon
www.amazon.jobs/en
View and apply for positions at Amazon all over the world.
FOCUS: Professional, customer service, fulfillment centers

CashCrate.com
www.cashcrate.com
Make money online by testing products, taking surveys, and shopping online.
FOCUS: Product tester

Click Worker
www.clickworker.com/clickworker/?customer=false
Participate in surveys, edit text, or search and categorize data.
FOCUS: Writing, survey taking, data analysis/aggregation, web research

CookUnity
www.cookunity.com/become-a-chef/
Become a part-time chef in NYC.
FOCUS: Cooking

Home Advisor

www.homeadvisor.com

Create a profile, list your services, and bid on projects that fit your skillset and timeline.

FOCUS: Home Improvement

Slice the Pie

www.slicethepie.com

Get paid to share your opinion on music tracks and clothing.

FOCUS: Reviews

PricewaterhouseCoopers Talent Exchange

https://talentexchange.pwc.com

Get matched with PwC opportunities that match your skillset.

FOCUS: Development, design, education

Thumbtack

www.thumbtack.com

Create a profile, list your services, and bid on projects.

FOCUS: Home Improvement, design, marketing, healthcare

Thumbtack

www.thumbtack.com

Create a profile, list your services, and bid on projects.

FOCUS: Home Improvement, design, marketing, healthcare

Workamper

www.workamper.com

Work for RV campers.

FOCUS: Culinary, field reps, transporation, entertainment

SECTION 7
SPECIALTY PROFESSIONS

Although there are fewer specialty profession sites available, this is area where tremendous growth is expected. Tele-health advances make it possible for medical personnel to operate differently. Smaller companies are looking for legal advice on an ad-hoc basis because they can't afford a retainer. And, engineers can consult on projects any place in the world.

Opportunities include 3-D modeling, architecture, various engineering work, health and medical work and legal services. Most of the websites are job boards.

Aerotek
www.aerotek.com
Find and apply for tech and engineering jobs.
FOCUS: Engineering, administrative, IT, scientific, skilled trade

All Medical Personnel
www.allmedstaffing.com
A job board for healthcare related positions throughout the United States.
FOCUS: Healthcare

Exec Searches
https://execsearches.com
View and apply for non-profit jobs in various industries and functions.
FOCUS: Non-profit

Field Engineer
www.fieldengineer.com
Find and bid on engineering jobs that fit your skillset and schedule.
FOCUS: Engineering

Fonemed
www.fonemed.com/wordpress
Communications and customer service positions in the healthcare industry.
FOCUS: Communications, customer service

Health eCareers
www.healthecareers.com
Find and apply for positions in the healthcare industry.
FOCUS: Healthcare

Health Jobs Nationwide
www.healthjobsnationwide.com
A job board with various positions available in the healthcare industry.
FOCUS: Healthcare, IT, tech

Law Jobs
www.lawjobs.com
A job board for legal professionals.
FOCUS: Legal

LawMatch
attorney-jobs.lawmatch.com
A job board for legal professionals.
FOCUS: Legal

Legal Career Central
https://jobs.americanbar.org
Find legal positions in the United States across a variety of industry sectors.
FOCUS: Legal

The Lawyer Whisperer
www.thelawyerwhisperer.com
Find legal positions anywhere in the world across a variety of sectors.
FOCUS: Legal

SECTION 8
TECH

Technology gig opportunities are plentiful in the online marketplace. Job boards list available positions in artificial intelligence, cyber security, data management, gaming, mobile apps, networking, programming, quality assurance, software development, system administration and website development. Not only will you find tech jobs listed in this section, but you will also find them in the general and business sections because technology is so closely integrated with most of the work done these days.

Authentic Jobs
https://authenticjobs.com/
A job board for creative professionals. Positions range in skill level, location, and compensation.
FOCUS: Design, development, IT, and marketing

Dice
www.dice.com
A tech-focused job board with opportunities all over the United States.
FOCUS: Technology, web development

Github
https://jobs.github.com
A job board just for developers. Positions range from full-time, part-time, remote, or in-person.
FOCUS: Development

Krop
www.krop.com
Look for freelance and full-time design/technology-focused jobs.
FOCUS: Design, technology

Landing Jobs

www.landing.jobs
A job board for tech professionals.
FOCUS: Development, computer security, UX design

Ruby Now

https://jobs.rubynow.com/
A job board for Ruby on Rails developers.
FOCUS: Ruby developers

Smashing Jobs

https://jobs.smashingmagazine.com/jobs/
A job board for designers and developers. Find remote, in-person, part-time or full-time positions.
FOCUS: Design, development, programming

Software Judge

www.softwarejudge.com
Get paid to share your opinion on software.
FOCUS: Reviews

Sologig

www.sologig.com
Find IT and engineering positions in various industries throughout the United States.
FOCUS: IT, development, programming

Stack Overflow

www.stackoverflow.com
A job board for developers, programmers and IT professionals.
FOCUS: Development, IT, computer engineering, programming

User Testing

www.usertesting.com/be-a-user-tester
Make money online by testing apps.
FOCUS: App testing

SECTION 9
TUTORING

Tutoring jobs are available for test preparation as well as general academic courses for adults and children. Some of the gigs are in-person but most are online opportunities using white boards and/or video conferencing. Most websites will match you with students based on your areas of expertise. You may need to pass a proficiency and background check to work on some of the gig sites.

Brainfuse
www.brainfuse.com
Apply to be a tutor and start teaching students of all ages online.
FOCUS: Tutoring

Chegg Tutors
www.chegg.com/tutors/become-a-tutor/
Tutor students (of all ages) on various subjects to earn as little or a much as you want!
FOCUS: Tutoring

Homework Tutoring
www.homeworktutoring.com
Tutor students of all ages in a variety of subjects.
FOCUS: Tutoring

Online Tutoring
www.tutor.com
Become an online tutor and help students of all age levels.
FOCUS: Tutoring

TutorVista
www.tutorvista.com
Work from home as an online tutor.
FOCUS: Tutoring

Wyzant
www.wyzant.com/jobsearch
Apply to be a tutor, bid on projects and teach students of all ages on a variety of subjects.
FOCUS: Tutoring

SECTION 10
WRITING & TRANSLATION

On the internet, content is king. Therefore gig websites for writers are numerous. Jobs are available for academic writing, blogging, business writing, copywriting, creative writing, editing, proposal writing, and web content. The need for translation services is growing exponentially as our nation continues to transform into a global economy. Most of these positions are remote. Although there is only one gig site listed that specifically hires translators, check in the general category for many more opportunities. Similarly, many additional writing jobs are found in the general section.

Academic Writers Online
www.academicwritersonline.com
Work from home writing, editing, and proofreading content on topics you like. Bid on projects allowing you flexibility to work as much or as little as you prefer.
FOCUS: *Writing, editing, proofreading*

Blogging Jobs
www.bloggingpro.com/jobs
Job board for freelancers interested in blogging, writing, and editing in a variety of industries.
FOCUS: *Blogging, editing, writing*

Cricket Media
www.cricketmag.submittable.com/submit
Contribute your writing and illustrations to award-winning children's magazines.
FOCUS: *Writing, illustration*

Freelance Writing

www.freelancewriting.com/jobs

Freelance writing jobs available in a variety of industries. Positions range from contract, part-time, and full-time to remote and in-person.

FOCUS: Writing, journalism, editing

Freelance Writing Jobs

www.freelancewritinggigs.com

Freelance writing jobs available in a variety of industries.

FOCUS: Writing, editing

Journalism Jobs

www.journalismjobs.com

A job board for journalism related positions.

FOCUS: Journalism

Online Writing Jobs

www.online-writing-jobs.com

A job board for freelance writing jobs.

FOCUS: Writing, editing, proofreading

TechWriters

www.techwriters.com

A job board for tech writers. Find writing opportunties and apply.

FOCUS: Writing

Unbabel

www.unbabel.com/translators

Become a translator and claim projects right from your home.

FOCUS: Translation

WOW! Women On Writing

www.wow-womenonwriting.com

Find open writing opportunities and submit your work for publication.

FOCUS: Writing

BONUS MATERIALS

Tips for Doing the Hustle with Millennial Children

Some people over the age of 45 are challenged when it comes to technology. They don't feel comfortable and sometimes get confused about which tab to click. I even heard one woman say, "I don't want to break the internet." I hope she was only joking.

One way to deal with this fear is to work with your millennial children, or other family members, who are digital natives. Your children know that you can't break the internet and they learn new software quickly. With their help; your learning curve can drastically decrease and you will be better prepared to expand your operation.

I know it might feel uncomfortable to ask your children for help, but remember they have a vested interest in your success. Below are just a few reasons why they should be willing to work with you:

- Preserve their inheritance. The more money you earn, the more you can save and invest. So in essence, they would be working to invest in their own future financial security.
- Maintain a place to live. Unfortunately, about a third of millennials reside with their parents. They

simply cannot afford to secure their own apartments and homes. Helping to maintain a place to live is especially important if you have been laid off or are under-employed.

- Pay the college bills. Again, if you are unemployed or under-employed, your child might need to drop out of college. They can consider helping you succeed as an internship.
- Keep the baby sitter happy. If you are a regular baby sitter or provide backup care, your children want to keep you happy. When you help them and they help you, everyone is happy.
- Become aware of opportunities. As they help you, it is very possible that they will find their own quarter-life opportunity. You may very well introduce them to their new side hustle.
- Show love and support. Ultimately, the real reason why they should help you is because they love you and support your progress. That's what loved ones do.

Sometimes, millennial children don't have patience to work with mature learners. I can't tell you how many times my son has literally snatched some equipment out of my hands and said, "Let me just do it." It's important that you do not become dependent on them. They simply need to be patient until you can do it yourself or until you make enough money to hire someone else to do the things you prefer not to do.

If you can work with millennials, it is a beautiful marriage bringing together your wisdom and life experience with their technology prowess. Here are some suggestions on how millennials can work with you in the online gig world:

- Teach you. They can help you master the website by learning tasks that challenge you and teaching you how to complete them.
- Promote you. Ask your millennial helpers to share your gig work with everyone that they know. Word of mouth is a great promotional tool.
- Manage your social media. Setting up your social media sites, if needed, and managing the accounts will help to build your thought leadership. They can also assist you with placing ads on social sites.
- Find useful apps and software for you. There are so many free and inexpensive tools that can help you. The millennials could spend some time specifically seeking them out.
- Encourage you. If your money making venture takes off slower than expected, a few hugs and words of encouragement go a long way.

Mentoring and Training Programs from TKC Incorporated

At TKC Incorporated, we teach experienced mature workers how to earn income using what they already know. Through on-line training and in-person workshops, workers age 45 and older discover and launch their mid-life opportunity.

Our proprietary **Solo Launch Pad** is a step-by-step process, through which we guide you as you transform your talents, skills and passions into profit by leveraging simple 21st century technology.

Below are five offerings that might benefit you. Visit www.AngelaHeathSpeaks.com for further details.

- **Simplify**
  A two-part webinar that guides participants in identifying and packaging their talents, skills and passions for the marketplace.
- **Multiply**
  A six-part training that builds confidence, clarifies your offering, and confirms whether people will buy your product or service before you launch so you don't waste your time, effort, and money.
- **Magnify**
  Eight-week accountability groups for people who have already launched their money-making venture and are interested in growth. During this training, you develop a growth plan. You also learn shortcuts on how to make things happen. Because there is only one industry representative in each accountability group, members refer and truly support one another as they learn.
- **BOOM Conference**
  This one-day live event brings together people age 45 and older to learn how to start and grow businesses along with resource organizations that can help them. The BOOM Conference travels to cities where sponsors are available.

Leveraging the Gig Economy: Training for career professionals and coaches is a four-part training that increases your knowledge and skills to better prepare your clients for gig work. This training builds upon your existing career assessment activities and expands their implications to the gig economy. You will learn a sequential process that empowers and guides your clients as they consider three new options to earn income, while your job placement rates soar.

Digital Resources for Gig Workers

The following are a few free or nearly free resources that you might find helpful. To use gig websites you won't necessarily need all of them. However, in planning for your success, I have including them to help you grow!

- Canva (https://about.canva.com) Graphic design software.
- Docracy (https://www.docracy.com) Legal documents socially curated and shared.
- Dropbox (https://www.dropbox.com/individual) Cloud storage.
- Freecamp (https://freedcamp.com) Project planning tool.
- Freelance Facelift (https://www.freelancelift.com) Community offering training and information for freelancers.
- Freelancers Union (https://www.freelancersunion.org) A community offering benefits and information for freelancers.
- Google Calendar (https://calendar.google.com) On-line calendar.
- Hootsuite (https://hootsuite.com/plans/free#) Manage social media postings.
- Hubstaff (https://hubstaff.com) Time tracker.

- Law Guru (https://www.lawguru.com) Attorneys answer legal questions for free.
- Mailchimp (https://mailchimp.com) Email service.
- Mint (https://www.mint.com) Money management tool.
- PayPal (https://www.mint.com) Tool for purchasing and sending money online.
- ScoopIt (https://www.scoop.it) Information curator.

About the Author

Angela Heath is an award-winning entrepreneur, gig economy expert and keynote speaker. She is on a mission to simplify 21st century solutions for small businesses, career coaches and everyday people. Angela teaches how to earn more money and waste less time by leveraging the tools and talents found in the gig economy.

When Angela's son was diagnosed with leukemia twice, she could not work for years. She learned how to "do the hustle" using technology and gig work and now teaches low-hassle strategies to people 45 and older. In addition, she works with career professionals and coaches to help them better guide their clients in the new world of work.